Learn Basic A

Fast & I

Logan Musil, CPA

ISBN-13: 978-1515193166

www.learnaccountingeasy.com

To

Mighty Spirit Girl

Contents

Introduction

Wouldn't it be great if learning basic accounting was fast and easy?

That's what this short book is all about.

Fast—60 minutes or less.
Easy—like keeping score.
Bite-sized lessons.
Simple illustrations.
No prerequisites.

Here's the game plan:

~ SECTION 1: A ONE-HOUR CRASH COURSE ~

In section 1 you learn basic accounting in an hour or less. You can skip to just what you want to learn, such as debits and credits, or can invest the whole hour and learn all the topics. You can stop here if you like, or move on to section 2 for a closer look at basic accounting.

Chapter 1: Purpose of Accounting

We spend a moment to cover the overall purpose of accounting. Everything else builds on this.

- *Lesson 1: Purpose of Accounting*

Chapter 2: A Team Points Analogy

In lessons 2-5 we learn the basics of accounting by building on what you *already* know—how to add up points scored by a team! We add up points for a few games, and before you know it you've mastered accounts, ledgers, double-entry accounting and the accounting equation! We're getting set up to switch gears to real-world accounting in chapter 3, where points become dollars. Before long you'll be a pro at basic accounting!

- *Lesson 2: Accounts & Ledgers*
- *Lesson 3: Double-Entry Accounting*
- *Lesson 4: The Accounting Equation*
- *Lesson 5: Financial Statements*

Chapter 3: Real-World Accounting

In lessons 6-9, with the Team Points Analogy fresh on our minds at the end of lesson 5, we transition to real-world accounting. (1) Overall team points, (2) points scored by your teammates, and (3) points scored by you become (1) assets, (2) liabilities (debts), and (3) owners' equity. Each of these accounting terms are illustrated with simple definitions and examples. Armed with the understanding of what these terms mean and how they fit together, we learn how to record real-world business transactions. We also learn how to prepare the most important financial statements, to show summaries of the business transactions we've recorded over time.

- *Lesson 6: Accounts & Ledgers, Double-Entry Accounting, & The Accounting Equation*
- *Lesson 7: How to Record Transactions using the Accounting Equation & Double-Entry Accounting*
- *Lesson 8: How to Prepare Financial Statements (Balance Sheet & Income Statement)*
- *Lesson 9: General Ledger Accounts & the Chart of Accounts*

Chapter 4: Debits & Credits

Lessons 2-9 gave us a solid grasp of core accounting topics using plusses and minuses. By lessons 10-13, we're ready to learn how to use debits and credits to record business transactions, rather than plusses and minuses. We see that preparing the financial statements from debits and credits is very easy. We conclude with a quick reference chart for debits and credits that makes it easy to recall how to use debits and credits to record every type of transaction.

- *Lesson 10: Intro to Debits & Credits*
- *Lesson 11: How to use Debits & Credits to Record Transactions & Prepare Financial Statements (Balance Sheet & Income Statement)*
- *Lesson 12: Debits & Credits – Quick Reference*

~ SECTION 2: A CLOSER LOOK ~

Section 2 takes a closer look at basic accounting. It covers much of the same concepts covered in section 1 in greater depth. For example, in Section 1 you learn how transactions are first recorded in journals and later summarized in financial statements, like the balance sheet and income statement. Section 2 expands on this by showing you the "middle step" between the initial journal entries recording and the financial statements: the trial balance. Trial balance is just a fancy term for a list of account balances at a point in time—it'll be an easy learn by the time we get here.

Section 2 introduces new concepts such as accrual accounting, where we adjust revenues and expenses for transactions where cash isn't going in or out the door at the same time. We learn the third and fourth of the four major financial statements (statement of retained earnings and statement of cash flows). Again, no need to worry. By the time we get there these items will make perfect sense.

Here's the game plan for Section 2:

<u>Chapter 5: Building Blocks of Financial Statements</u>

Transaction Analysis

- Transaction
- Account
- Record
- Journal

Double-Entry Accounting

Accounting Equation

Ledger, General Ledger, Chart of Accounts, & Trial Balance

- Ledger
- Posting
- General ledger
- Trial balance (TB)
    - Unadjusted trial balance (TB)
    - Adjusted trial balance (TB)

Debits & Credits

- T-Accounts

Chapter 6: Accrual Accounting

Accrual accounting

- Revenue recognition principle
- Matching Principle
- Accruals
- Deferrals
- Adjusting Entries
    - Accrual adjustments
        - Record Accrued Revenues
        - Record Accrued Expenses
    - Deferral adjustments.
        - Adjust Deferred Revenues
        - Adjust Deferred Expenses
            - Depreciation

Chapter 7: Financial Statements

- Income Statement
- Statement of Retained Earnings
- Balance Sheet
- Statement of Cash Flows

Summary Diagrams

A tour from building blocks of financial statements to the financial statements

SECTION 1: ONE-HOUR CRASH COURSE

Chapter 1: Purpose of Accounting

We spend a moment to cover the overall purpose of accounting. Everything else builds on this.

Lesson 1: Purpose of Accounting

The overall purpose of accounting is to *provide information for making decisions*. As shown below, two major categories of information accounting is concerned with are financial *position* and financial *performance*.

Financial *Position* **as of a** **point in time** (e.g. 1/1/13).

- **Assets.** Stuff the organization owns
- **Liabilities**. The organization's debts
- **Owners' Equity.** Assets minus liabilities. *(In other words, money left over when liabilities are subtracted from assets.)*

Financial *Performance* over a **period of time** (e.g. 1/1/13 through 12/31/13).

- **Revenues.** The organization's **sales** of goods and services **to customers.**
- **Expenses**. The organization's **use** of goods and services **from vendors**.

- **<u>Net Income</u>**: Revenues minus expenses. *(In other words, profit.)*

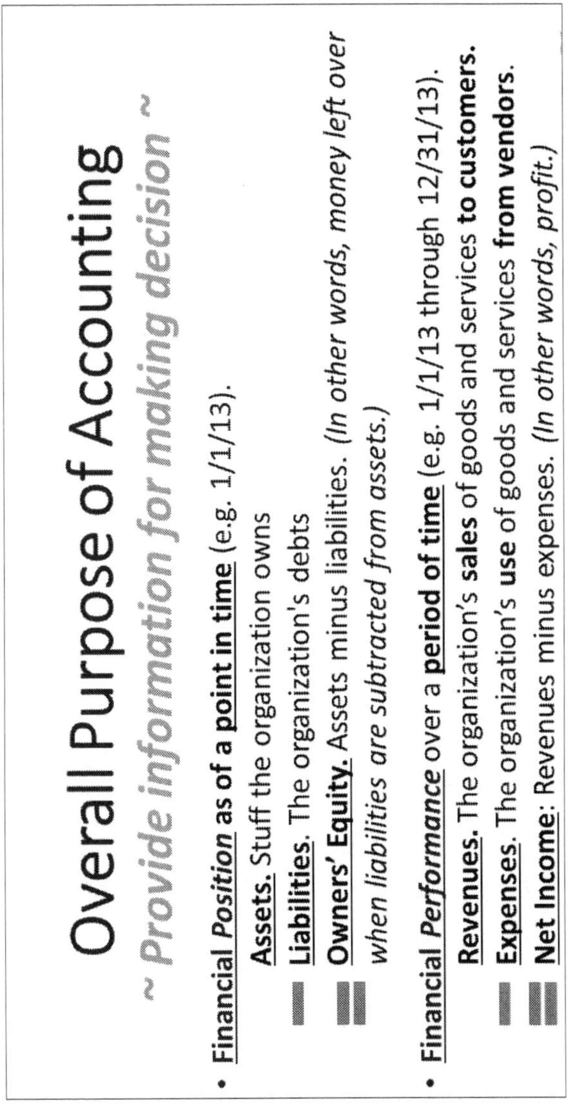

Overall Purpose of Accounting

~ Provide information for making decision ~

- **Financial *Position* as of a point in time** (e.g. 1/1/13).
  - **Assets.** Stuff the organization owns
  - **Liabilities.** The organization's debts
  - **Owners' Equity.** Assets minus liabilities. *(In other words, money left over when liabilities are subtracted from assets.)*
- **Financial *Performance*** over a **period of time** (e.g. 1/1/13 through 12/31/13).
  - **Revenues.** The organization's **sales** of goods and services **to customers.**
  - **Expenses.** The organization's **use** of goods and services **from vendors.**
  - **Net Income**: Revenues minus expenses. *(In other words, profit.)*

Figure 1

Chapter 2: Team Points Analogy

In lessons 2-5 we learn the basics of accounting by building on what you *already* know—how to add up points scored by a team! We add up points for a few games, and before you know it you've mastered accounts, ledgers, double-entry accounting and the accounting equation! We're getting set up to switch gears to real-world accounting in chapter 3, where points become dollars. Before long you'll be a pro at basic accounting!

- *Lesson 2: Accounts & Ledgers*
- *Lesson 3: Double-Entry Accounting*
- *Lesson 4: The Accounting Equation*
- *Lesson 5: Financial Statements*

Lesson 2: Accounts & Ledgers

Before we jump into real-world accounting, we'll spend a few minutes with a team points analogy to introduce some core accounting concepts. We'll start with accounts and ledgers.

What we see below in Figure 2 is simply a record of team points earned throughout the season. Each game has its own row. For each game, we need to record the points the team *as a whole* scored in the amount column. In the balance column we'll keep track of the running total of points throughout the season.

An *account* is a record of something. It can be thought of as a bucket for measuring something over time, as we see below in Figure 3. We also see that the document we use to measure an account balance over time is called a *ledger*. In this chapter accounts are used to keep track of team points, and in later chapters they will be used to keep track of dollars, just as they do in the real world.

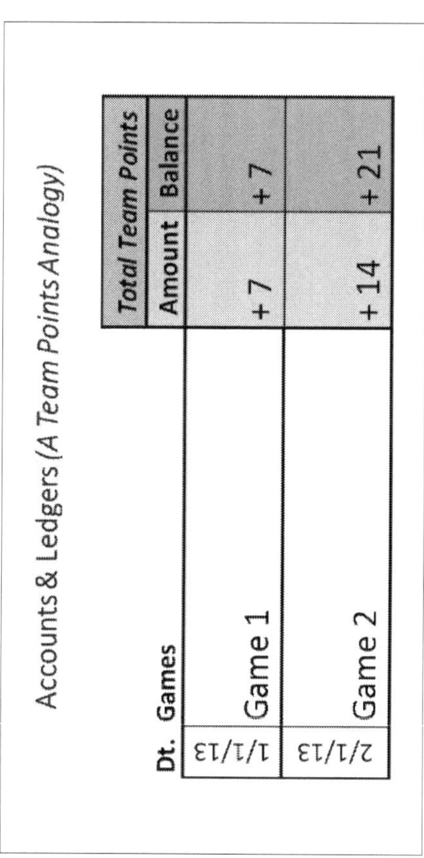

Accounts & Ledgers (*A Team Points Analogy*)

Dt.	Games	*Total Team Points*	
		Amount	Balance
1/1/13	Game 1	+ 7	+ 7
2/1/13	Game 2	+ 14	+ 21

Figure 2

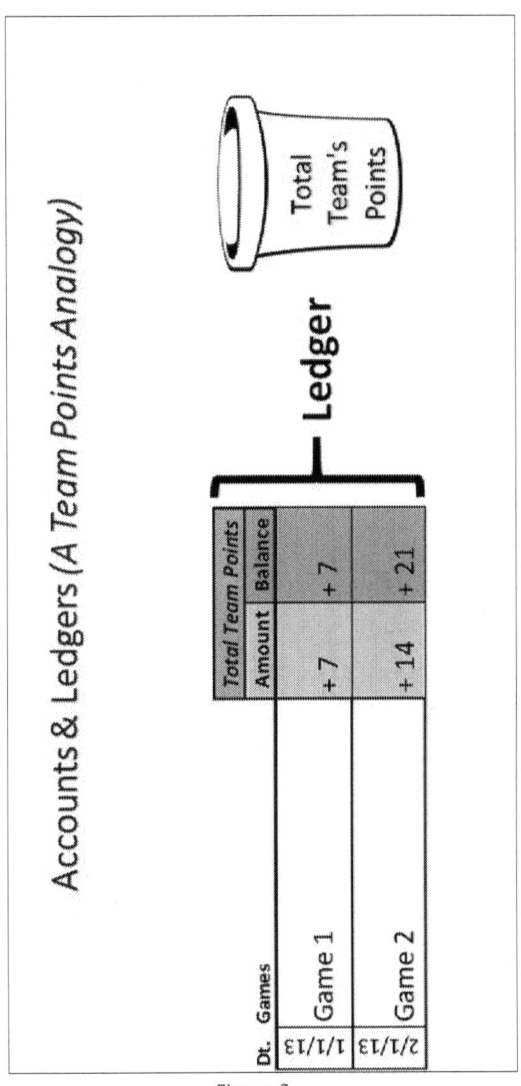

Dt.	Games	Total Team Points Amount	Total Team Points Balance
1/1/13	Game 1	+ 7	+ 7
2/1/13	Game 2	+ 14	+ 21

Figure 3

Lesson 3: Double-Entry Accounting

Double-entry accounting is a core concept in accounting. It basically says that if we want to record one event from multiple perspectives, we have to make multiple entries. We can use our team points analogy to introduce this concept. In lesson 2, we recorded team points as a whole for each game. We can add to that another perspective for each game: *Who has claim to those points?*

As Figure 4 shows, if, in addition to recording points as a whole for each game, we use newly created accounts to record “Others’ Points” and “My Points,” separately for each game, we are performing a form of double-entry accounting. For each game, we are recording:

- Total Team Points
- Who has claim to those points

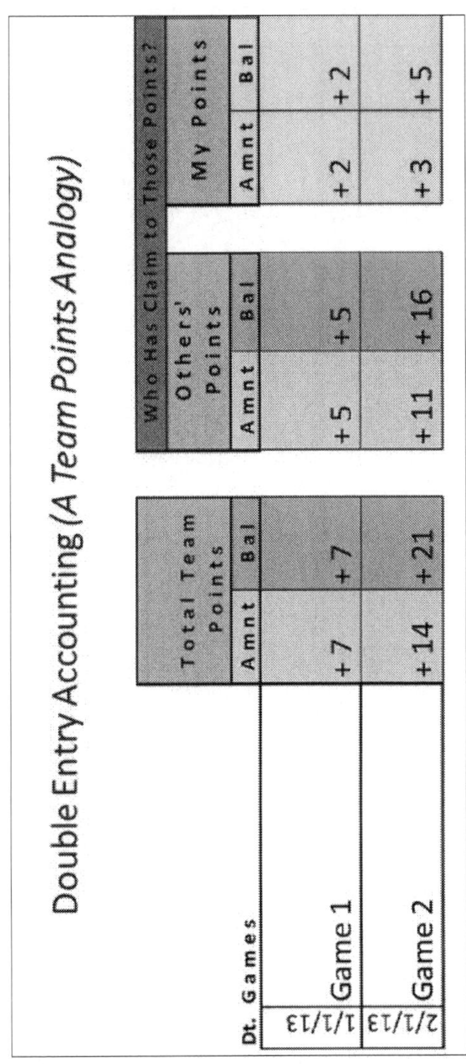

Double Entry Accounting *(A Team Points Analogy)*

Dt.	Games	Total Team Points		Who Has Claim to Those Points? Others' Points		My Points	
		Amnt	Bal	Amnt	Bal	Amnt	Bal
1/1/13	Game 1	+7	+7	+5	+5	+2	+2
2/1/13	Game 2	+14	+21	+11	+16	+3	+5

Figure 4

Lesson 4: The Accounting Equation

As Figure 5 shows, we create a form of an *accounting equation* by adding to Figure 4:

- An equals sign between the left side – "Total Team Points"—and the right side—"Who Has claim to those points?"; and
- A plus sign between "Others' Points" and "My Points."

Why does Figure 5 represent a form of an accounting equation? *Because the left side has to equal the right side.* This will be true with our team points analogy, and also in following chapters when we have moved into real-world accounting.

The left side has to equal the right side because each side is recording the *same exact events* (games), just from multiple perspectives. This will be the case when we move on to real-world accounting in following chapters. Instead of games, the events will be business transactions measured in dollars, like the sale of a service to a customer.

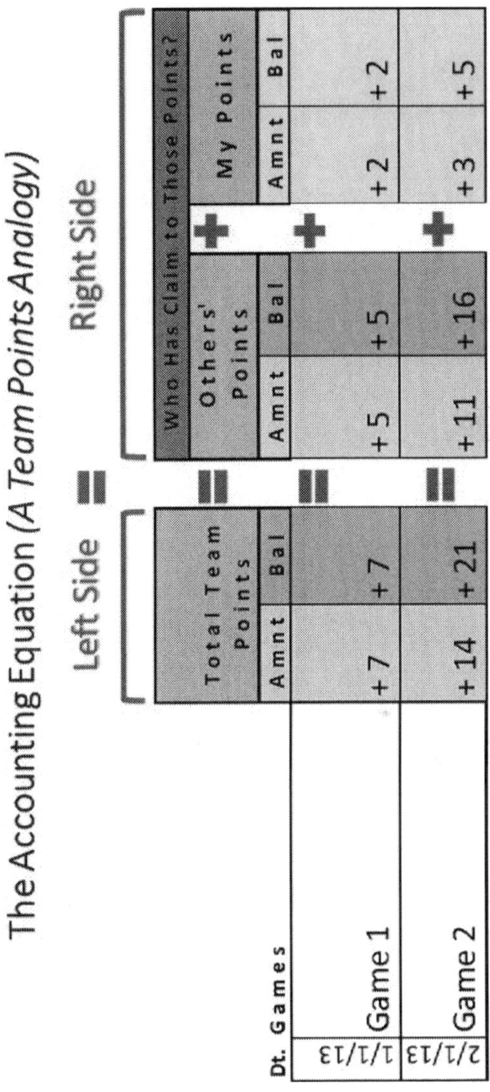
The Accounting Equation *(A Team Points Analogy)*
Left Side
=
Right Side
Who Has Claim to Those Points?
Total Team Points
Others' Points
My Points
Dt.
Games
Amnt
Bal
Amnt
Bal
Amnt
Bal
1/1/13
Game 1
+ 7
+ 7
+ 5
+ 5
+ 2
+ 2
2/1/13
Game 2
+ 14
+ 21
+ 11
+ 16
+ 3
+ 5

Figure 5

Lesson 5: Financial Statements

We can use our team points analogy to introduce the concept of financial statements—the balance sheet and the income statement.

"Team Points as of 2/1/13" – It's like a Balance Sheet

See the bottom-left box in Figure 6 below. We see that the "Team Points as of 2/1/13" Report is summarizing everything we've accounted for *as of* 2/1/13, so games 1 and 2. "Total team points" shows up at the top. "Others' points" and "my points" show up at the bottom. Notice how this just turns the accounting equation 90 degrees. Also notice how this report covers a *point* in time rather than a *period* of time. This report looks like the balance sheet in the next chapter, which summarizes dollars as of a point in time.

"My Points from 1/1/13 – 2/1/13"– It's like an Income Statement

See the bottom-right box in Figure 6 below. We see that the "My Points from 1/1/13 – 2/1/13" Report is summarizing only "My Points," for the entire season, so games 1 and 2. Notice how this report covers a *period* of time rather than a *point* in time. This report looks like the income statement in the next chapter, which summarizes dollars over a period of time.

Another similarity between the bottom-right box in Figure 6 below and the income statement in the next chapter is that each summarize only a *portion* of the accounts we've kept track of. In our team points example, we were only concerned with the "My Points" account to create the "My Points from 1/1/13 – 2/1/13" Report. With the income statement in the next chapter, we will be summarizing *only* revenue and expense accounts, because they make up net income, the "bottom line" of the income statement.

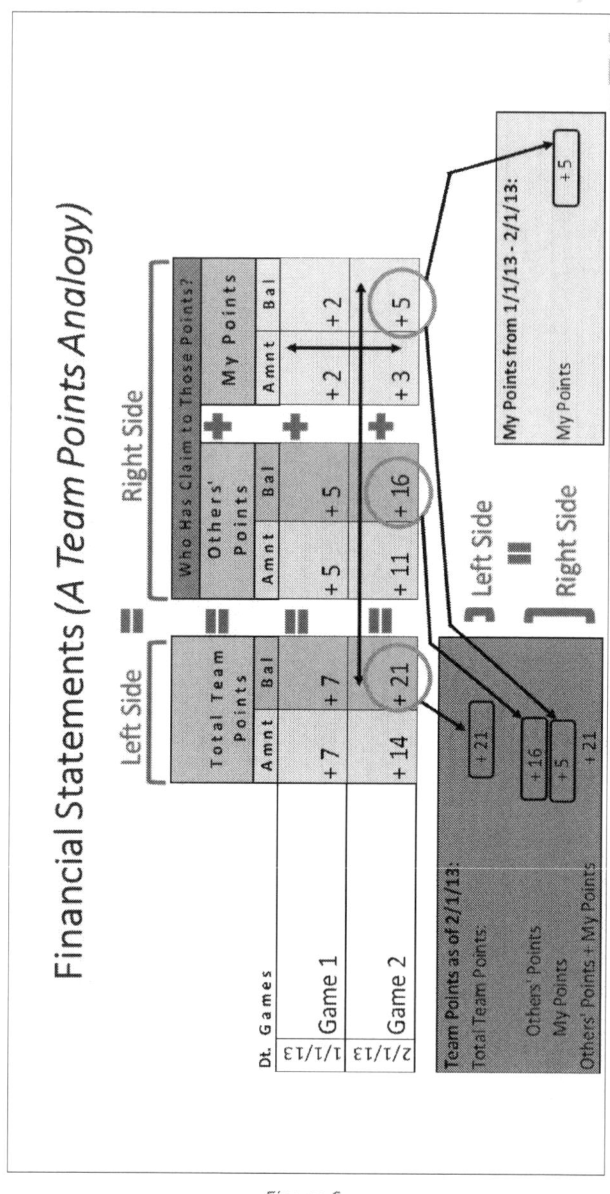
Financial Statements (A Team Points Analogy)
Left Side
Right Side
Who Has Claim to Those Points?
Dt.
Games
Total Team Points
Others' Points
My Points
Amnt
Bal
1/1/13
Game 1
+ 7
+ 7
+ 5
+ 5
+ 2
+ 2
2/1/13
Game 2
+ 14
+ 21
+ 11
+ 16
+ 3
+ 5
Team Points as of 2/1/13:
Total Team Points:
+ 21
Others' Points
+ 16
My Points
+ 5
Others' Points + My Points
+ 21
Left Side
=
Right Side
My Points from 1/1/13 - 2/1/13:
My Points
+ 5

Figure 6

Chapter 3: Real-World Accounting

In lessons 6-9, with the Team Points Analogy fresh on our minds at the end of lesson 5 in chapter 2, we transition to real-world accounting. As we see below in Figure 7, (1) Overall team points, (2) points scored by your teammates, and (3) points scored by you become (1) assets, (2) liabilities (or debts), and (3) owners' equity. Each of these accounting terms are illustrated with simple definitions and examples. Armed with the understanding of what these terms represent and how they fit together, we learn how to record real-world business transactions. We also learn how to prepare financial statements, the balance sheet and the income statement, to show summaries of the transactions we've recorded over time.

- *Lesson 6: Accounts & Ledgers, Double-Entry Accounting, & The Accounting Equation*
- *Lesson 7: How to Record Transactions using the Accounting Equation & Double-Entry Accounting*
- *Lesson 8: How to Prepare Financial Statements (Balance Sheet & Income Statement)*
- *Lesson 9: General Ledger Accounts & the Chart of Accounts*

Lesson 6: Accounts & Ledgers, Double-Entry Accounting, & The Accounting Equation

As we see below in Figure 7, (1) Overall team points, (2) points scored by your teammates, and (3) points scored by you become (1) assets, (2) liabilities (or debts), and (3) owners' equity. Notice how, as we switch to the real-world accounting equation at the bottom half of Figure 7, the left side asks, "What are total assets?" and the right side asks, "Who has claim to those assets?" And just as the right side of the team points accounting equation (top half of Figure 7) was divided into two groups of people – your teammates and you, the real-world accounting equation's right side is divided into two groups:

- Liabilities: The amount owed to creditors (creditors are lenders; they are *outside the business* in that they are *not* owners), and
- Owners' equity: The amount of total assets left over for the business's owners after liabilities are deducted (total assets minus total liabilities)

For a refresher on definitions of assets, liabilities and owners' equity, see chapter 1. For a more in-depth look at these items, see section 2.

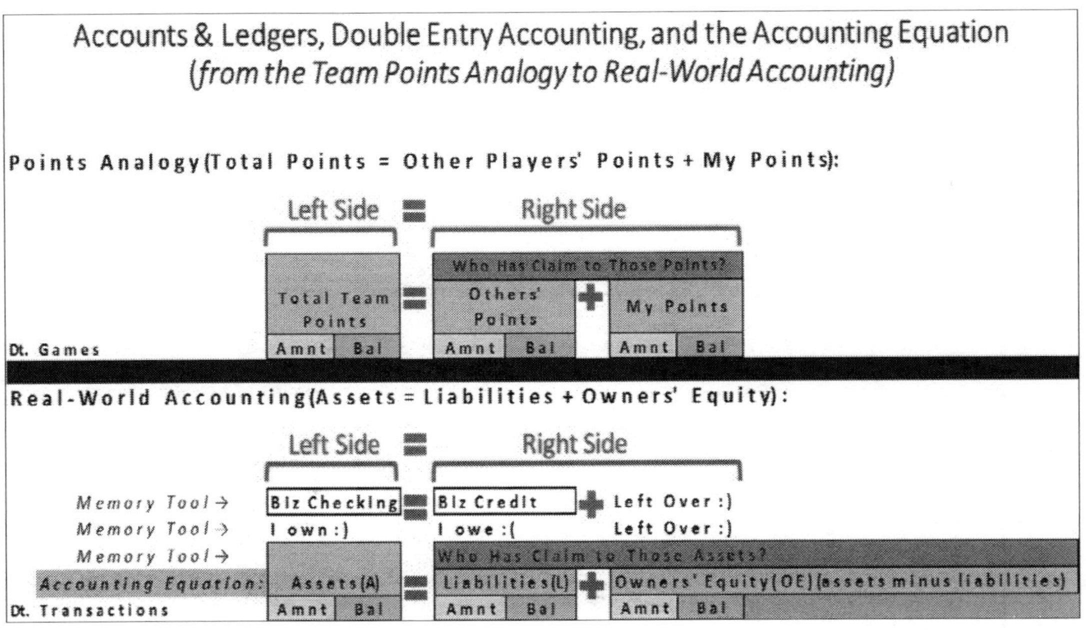
Accounts & Ledgers, Double Entry Accounting, and the Accounting Equation
(from the Team Points Analogy to Real-World Accounting)
Points Analogy(Total Points = Other Players' Points + My Points):
Left Side
=
Right Side
Who Has Claim to Those Points?
Total Team Points
=
Others' Points
+
My Points
Dt. Games
Amnt
Bal
Amnt
Bal
Amnt
Bal
Real-World Accounting(Assets = Liabilities + Owners' Equity):
Left Side
=
Right Side
Memory Tool →
Biz Checking
=
Biz Credit
+
Left Over :)
Memory Tool →
I own :)
I owe :(
Left Over :)
Memory Tool →
Who Has Claim to Those Assets?
Accounting Equation:
Assets(A)
=
Liabilities(L)
+
Owners' Equity(OE)(assets minus liabilities)
Dt. Transactions
Amnt
Bal
Amnt
Bal
Amnt
Bal

Figure 7

Lesson 7: How to Record Transactions using the Accounting Equation & Double-Entry Accounting

At this point we're ready to use the accounting equation and double-entry accounting to record our first set of transactions. By the end of this lesson we will have covered six very common types of transactions. We will use plusses and minuses in this lesson to record the transactions. In the next chapter we will use debits and credits to record the same transactions, and we will see this side-by-side with the plusses-and-minuses method.

1/1/13 Transaction:

The first transaction to record is in Figure 8. On 1/1/13 we received $1,000 in our business checking account from a business owner's personal checking account. The business owner is the owner of *our* business, the business we are accounting for in this example.

The first thing we can do is look to the left side of the accounting equation and ask, "What happened to total assets?" The answer is: Business cash went up by $1,000. So we put a "+1,000" in the assets account.

The next thing we can do is look to the right side of the accounting equation and ask, "Who has claim to those assets?" The answer is: The owners have claim to the $1,000. So we put a "+1,000" in the owners' equity account.

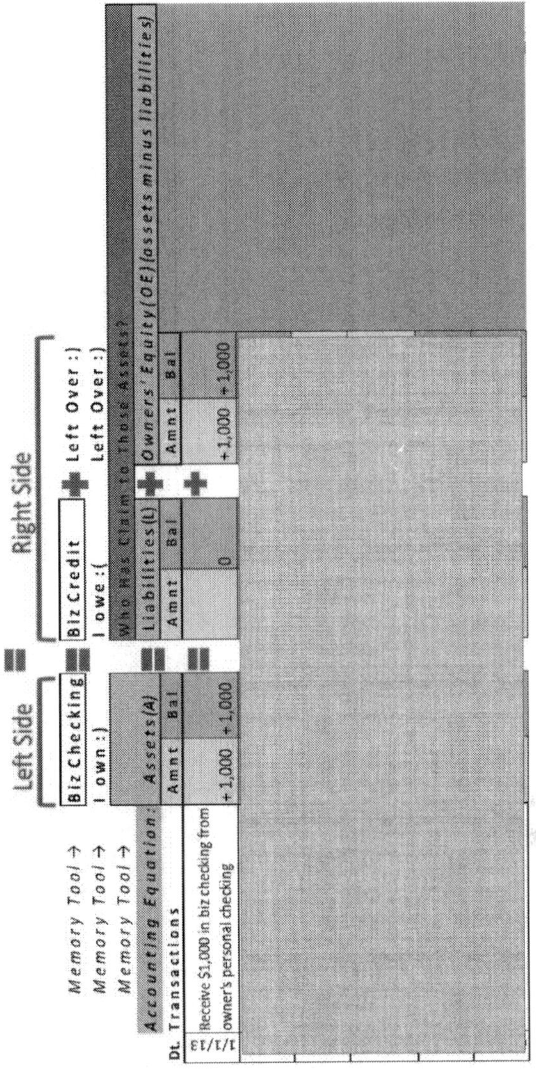
Left Side
=
Right Side
Memory Tool → Biz Checking = Biz Credit + Left Over :)
Memory Tool → I own :) I owe :(Left Over :)
Memory Tool → Who Has Claim to Those Assets?
Accounting Equation: Assets(A) = Liabilities(L) + Owners' Equity(OE)(assets minus liabilities)
Dt. Transactions Amnt Bal Amnt Bal Amnt Bal
1/1/13 Receive $1,000 in biz checking from owner's personal checking +1,000 +1,000 = 0 + +1,000 +1,000

Figure 8

2/1/13 Transaction:

The second transaction to record is in Figure 9. On 2/1/13 we received $500 in our business checking account by charging $500 on our business credit card. The lender, also called creditor, is the credit card company. Our new debt is also called a liability.

The first thing we can do is look to the left side of the accounting equation and ask, "What happened to total assets?" The answer is: Business cash went up by $500. So we put a "+500" in the assets account. We also notice that since we received $1,000 on 1/1/13 in the first transaction, we now have a cumulative total of $1,500 in business checking as of 2/1/13.

The next thing we can do is look to the right side of the accounting equation and ask, "Who has claim to those assets?" The answer is: The credit card company (a creditor) has claim to the $500. So we put a "+500" in the liabilities account.

We also notice how, since there was no owners' equity activity on 2/1/13, we simply carried forward the $1,000 owners' equity balance from 1/1/13 to 2/1/13.

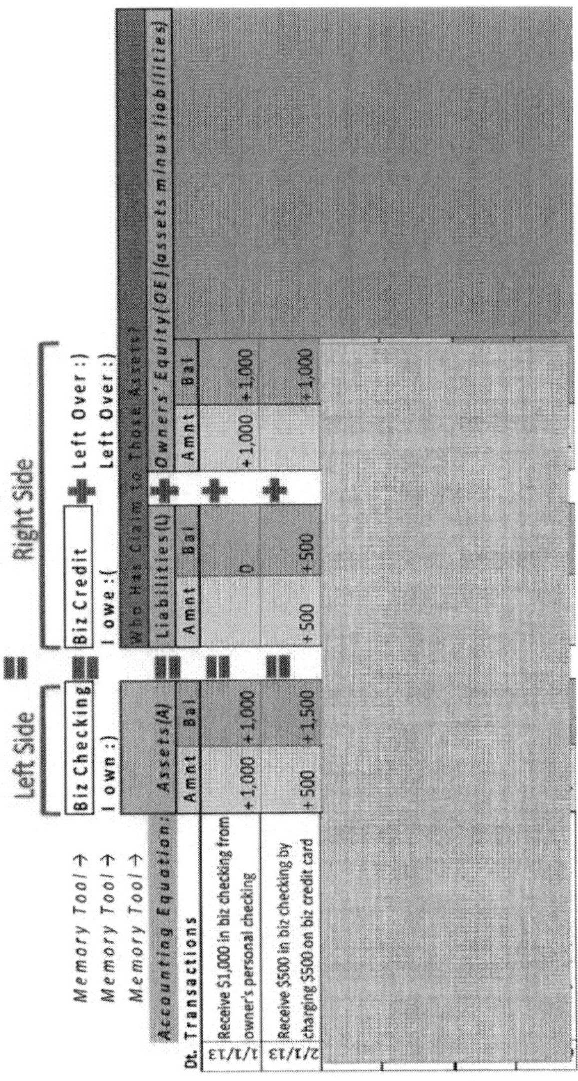

		Left Side		=	Right Side		+		
Memory Tool →		Biz Checking		=	Biz Credit		+	Left Over :)	
Memory Tool →		I own :)			I owe :(			Left Over :)	
Memory Tool →					Who Has Claim to Those Assets?				
Accounting Equation:		Assets(A)		=	Liabilities(L)		+	Owners' Equity(OE)(assets minus liabilities)	
Dt.	Transactions	Amnt	Bal		Amnt	Bal		Amnt	Bal
1/1/13	Receive $1,000 in biz checking from owner's personal checking	+1,000	+1,000	=		0	+	+1,000	+1,000
2/1/13	Receive $500 in biz checking by charging $500 on biz credit card	+500	+1,500	=	+500	+500	+		+1,000

Figure 9

3/1/13 Transaction:

The third transaction to record is in Figure 10. On 3/1/13 we paid $400 from our business checking account for coffee received from a vendor. We are considering this coffee a business expense.

The first thing we can do is look to the left side of the accounting equation and ask, "What happened to total assets?" The answer is: Business cash went down by $400. So we put a "- 400" in the assets account.

The next thing we can do is look to the right side of the accounting equation and ask, "Who has claim to those assets?" In this case the answer is that the owners owned $400 less in the business because of the expense. Stated a different way, owners' equity was reduced by $400. So we put a "- 400" in the owners' equity account. Another way we can think of this is: The owners took the burden of the $400 cash reduction. The transaction had nothing to do with paying off the credit card company, so we record nothing in the liabilities account.

We also notice how, since there were no liabilities activity on 3/1/13, we simply carried forward the $500 liabilities balance from 2/1/13 to 3/1/13.

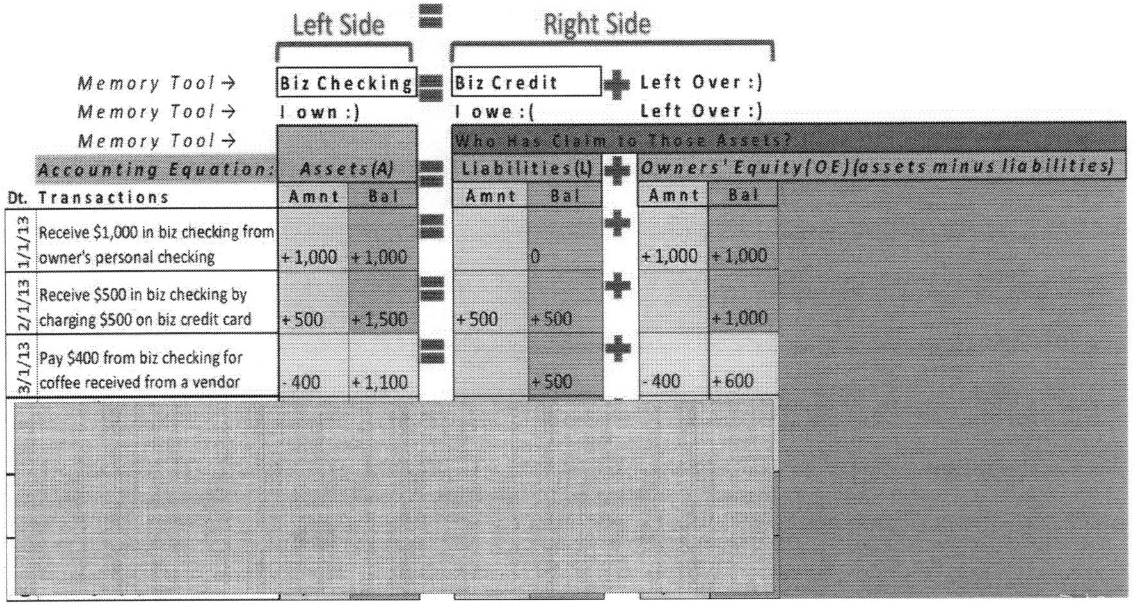

		Left Side		=	Right Side				
Memory Tool →		Biz Checking		=	Biz Credit		+	Left Over :)	
Memory Tool →		I own :)			I owe :(			Left Over :)	
Memory Tool →					Who Has Claim to Those Assets?				
Accounting Equation:		Assets(A)		=	Liabilities(L)		+	Owners' Equity(OE)(assets minus liabilities)	
Dt.	Transactions	Amnt	Bal		Amnt	Bal		Amnt	Bal
1/1/13	Receive $1,000 in biz checking from owner's personal checking	+1,000	+1,000	=		0	+	+1,000	+1,000
2/1/13	Receive $500 in biz checking by charging $500 on biz credit card	+500	+1,500	=	+500	+500	+		+1,000
3/1/13	Pay $400 from biz checking for coffee received from a vendor	-400	+1,100	=		+500	+	-400	+600

Figure 10

4/1/13 Transaction:

The fourth transaction to record is in Figure 11. On 4/1/13 we received $600 in our business checking account for legal services we performed for one of our customers. This is considered *revenue*.

The first thing we can do is look to the left side of the accounting equation and ask, "What happened to total assets?" The answer is: Business cash went up by $600. So we put a "+ 600" in the assets account.

The next thing we can do is look to the right side of the accounting equation and ask, "Who has claim to those assets?" The answer is: The owners' equity was increased by $600. So we put a "+600" in the owners' equity account. Another way we can think of this is: The owners received the benefit of the $600 cash inflow. The transaction had nothing to do with paying off the credit card company, so we record nothing in the liabilities account.

We also notice how, since there were no liabilities activity on 4/1/13, we simply carried forward the $500 liabilities balance from 3/1/13 to 4/1/13.

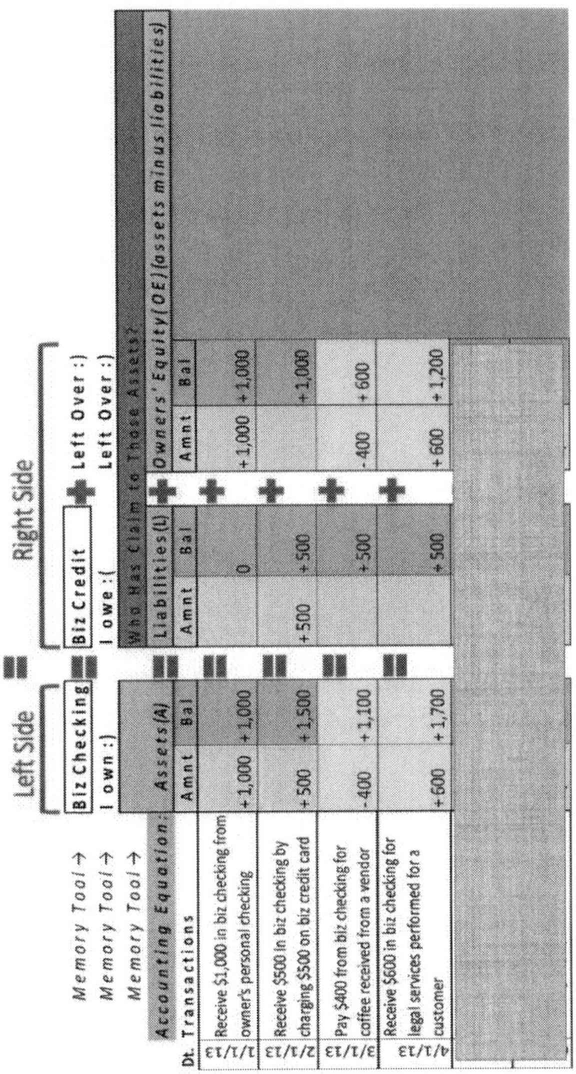

		Left Side		=	Right Side				
Memory Tool →		Biz Checking		=	Biz Credit		+	Left Over :)	
Memory Tool →		I own :)			I owe :(			Left Over :)	
Memory Tool →					Who Has Claim to Those Assets?				
Accounting Equation:		Assets(A)		=	Liabilities(L)		+	Owners' Equity(OE)(assets minus liabilities)	
Dt.	Transactions	Amnt	Bal		Amnt	Bal		Amnt	Bal
1/1/13	Receive $1,000 in biz checking from owner's personal checking	+1,000	+1,000	=		0	+	+1,000	+1,000
2/1/13	Receive $500 in biz checking by charging $500 on biz credit card	+500	+1,500	=	+500	+500	+		+1,000
3/1/13	Pay $400 from biz checking for coffee received from a vendor	-400	+1,100	=		+500	+	-400	+600
4/1/13	Receive $600 in biz checking for legal services performed for a customer	+600	+1,700	=		+500	+	+600	+1,200

Figure 11

5/1/13 Transaction:

The fifth transaction to record is in Figure 12. On 5/1/13 we used $500 from our business checking account to pay off our credit card balance.

The first thing we can do is look to the left side of the accounting equation and ask, "What happened to total assets?" The answer is: Business cash went down by $500. So we put a "- 500" in the assets account.

The next thing we can do is look to the right side of the accounting equation and ask, "Who has claim to those assets?" The answer is: The creditors received claim to the $500, as we paid them off. So we put a "-500" in the liabilities account, which brought the running balance down to zero.

We also notice how, since there was no owners' equity activity on 5/1/13, we simply carried forward the $1,200 owners' equity balance from 4/1/13 to 5/1/13.

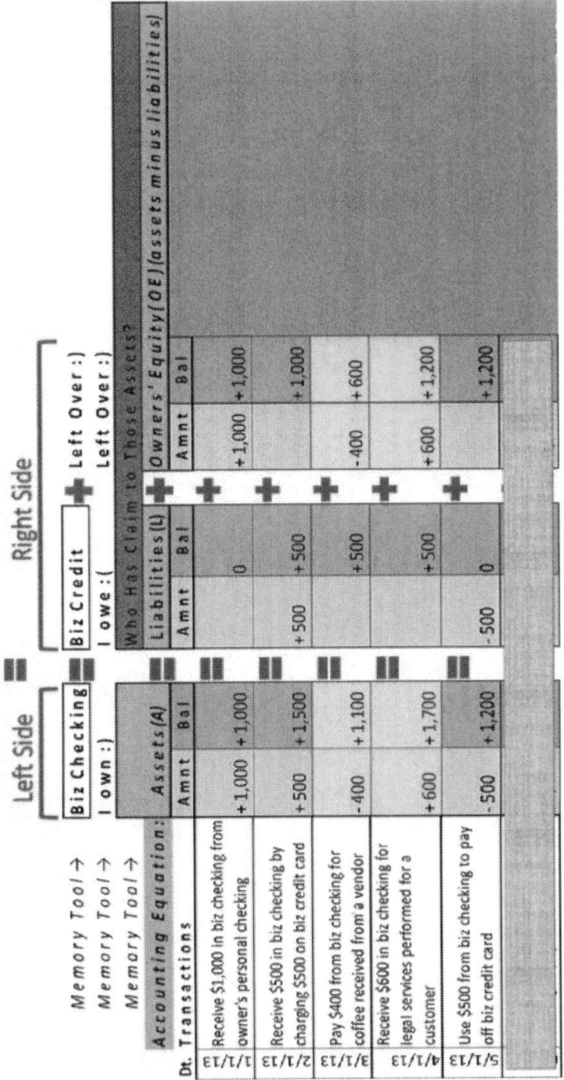

		Left Side		=	Right Side		+		
	Memory Tool →	Biz Checking		=	Biz Credit		+	Left Over :)	
	Memory Tool →	I own :)		=	I owe :(			Left Over :)	
	Memory Tool →				Who Has Claim to Those Assets?				
	Accounting Equation:	Assets(A)		=	Liabilities(L)		+	Owners' Equity(OE)(assets minus liabilities)	
Dt.	Transactions	Amnt	Bal	=	Amnt	Bal	+	Amnt	Bal
1/1/13	Receive $1,000 in biz checking from owner's personal checking	+1,000	+1,000	=		0	+	+1,000	+1,000
2/1/13	Receive $500 in biz checking by charging $500 on biz credit card	+500	+1,500	=	+500	+500	+		+1,000
3/1/13	Pay $400 from biz checking for coffee received from a vendor	-400	+1,100	=		+500	+	-400	+600
4/1/13	Receive $600 in biz checking for legal services performed for a customer	+600	+1,700	=		+500	+	+600	+1,200
5/1/13	Use $500 from biz checking to pay off biz credit card	-500	+1,200	=	-500	0	+		+1,200

Figure 12

6/1/13 Transaction:

The sixth and final transaction to record is in Figure 13. On 6/1/13 we withdrew all $1,200 from our business checking account to pay the business owners. This was considered a liquidation of the business, or a distribution of all the business's assets to its owners.

The first thing we can do is look to the left side of the accounting equation and ask, "What happened to total assets?" The answer is: Business cash went down by $1,200. So we put a "- 1,200" in the assets account. This brought the running cash balance down to zero. Remember that this is the *business* checking account. The $1,200 paid to the owners from the *business* checking ended up in the owners' *personal* bank accounts.

The next thing we can do is look to the right side of the accounting equation and ask, "Who has claim to those assets?" The answer is: The owners now have $1,200 less of ownership interest in the business. So we put a "- 1,200" in the owners' equity account, which brought the running balance down to zero.

We also notice how, since there were no liabilities activity on 6/1/13, we simply carried forward the $0 liabilities balance from 5/1/13 to 6/1/13.

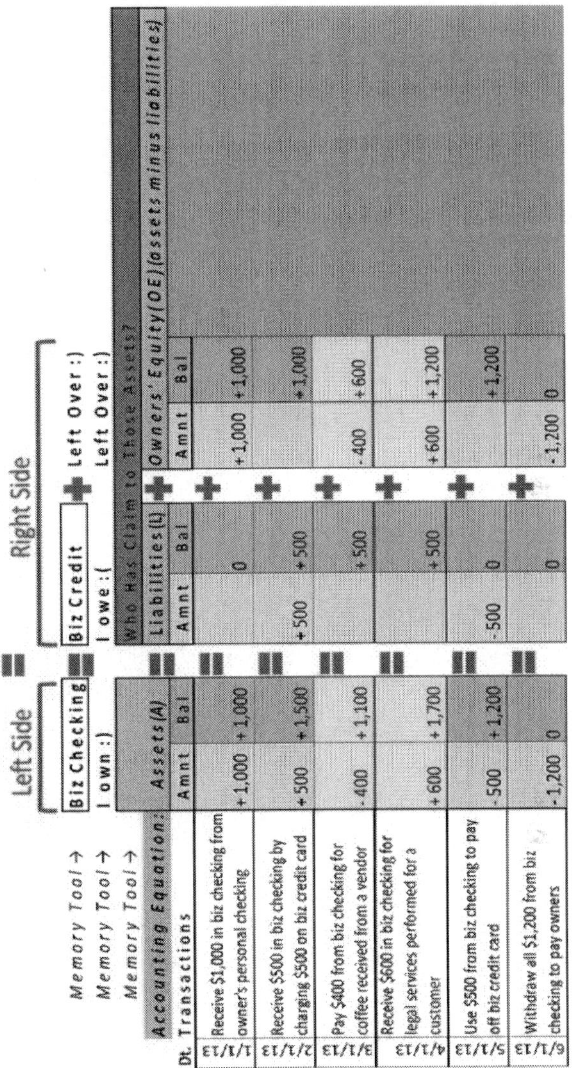

	Memory Tool →	Left Side		=	Right Side				
	Memory Tool →	Biz Checking		=	Biz Credit		+	Left Over :)	
	Memory Tool →	I own :)			I owe :(			Left Over :)	
	Accounting Equation:	Assets(A)		=	Who Has Claim to Those Assets? Liabilities(L)		+	Owners' Equity(OE)(assets minus liabilities)	
Dt.	Transactions	Amnt	Bal	=	Amnt	Bal	+	Amnt	Bal
1/1/13	Receive $1,000 in biz checking from owner's personal checking	+1,000	+1,000	=		0	+	+1,000	+1,000
2/1/13	Receive $500 in biz checking by charging $500 on biz credit card	+500	+1,500	=	+500	+500	+		+1,000
3/1/13	Pay $400 from biz checking for coffee received from a vendor	-400	+1,100	=		+500	+	-400	+600
4/1/13	Receive $600 in biz checking for legal services performed for a customer	+600	+1,700	=		+500	+	+600	+1,200
5/1/13	Use $500 from biz checking to pay off biz credit card	-500	+1,200	=	-500	0	+		+1,200
6/1/13	Withdraw all $1,200 from biz checking to pay owners	-1,200	0	=		0	+	-1,200	0

Figure 13

Dividing Owners' Equity into four accounts:

See Figure 14. Now that we have covered how to use the accounting equation and double-entry accounting to record our first set of transactions, we need to divide the owners' equity account into four accounts that affect owners' equity:

- Owner Investments
- Owner Withdrawals
- Revenues
- Expenses

In the real world, these specific types of transactions are recorded into these specific accounts, rather than one owners equity account.

We divided the owners' equity account into four accounts because we need this level of detail to produce the income statement. As discussed in chapter 1, the income statement shows revenues and expenses. We need separate accounts for revenues and expenses so that we can add up these account balances at the end of the year and calculate our net income, or profit. As discussed in chapter 1, profit equals revenues minus expenses. If we only had the "Owners' Equity" account to record transactions related to owner investments, owner withdrawals, revenues, and expenses, as if they were all the same kind of activity, we wouldn't have the level of detail needed to isolate just revenues and expenses, and prepare the income statement.

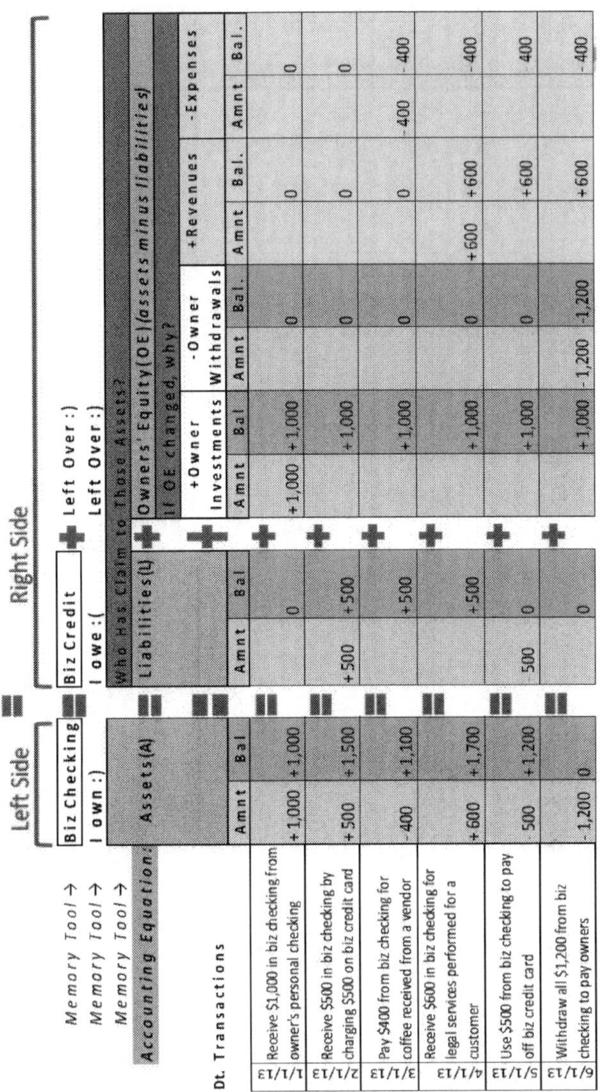

	Left Side		=	Right Side											
Memory Tool →	Biz Checking		=	Biz Credit		+	Left Over :)								
Memory Tool →	I own :)			I owe :(			Left Over :)								
Memory Tool →				Who Has Claim to Those Assets?											
Accounting Equation:	Assets(A)		=	Liabilities(L)		+	Owners' Equity(OE) *(assets minus liabilities)*								
							If OE changed, why?								
Dt. Transactions			=			+	+Owner Investments		-Owner Withdrawals		+Revenues		-Expenses		
	Amnt	Bal		Amnt	Bal		Amnt	Bal	Amnt	Bal.	Amnt	Bal.	Amnt	Bal.	
1/1/13 Receive $1,000 in biz checking from owner's personal checking	+1,000	+1,000	=		0	+	+1,000	+1,000		0		0		0	
2/1/13 Receive $500 in biz checking by charging $500 on biz credit card	+500	+1,500	=	+500	+500	+		+1,000		0		0		0	
3/1/13 Pay $400 from biz checking for coffee received from a vendor	- 400	+1,100	=		+500	+		+1,000		0		0	-400	- 400	
4/1/13 Receive $600 in biz checking for legal services performed for a customer	+600	+1,700	=		+500	+		+1,000		0	+600	+600		- 400	
5/1/13 Use $500 from biz checking to pay off biz credit card	- 500	+1,200	=	- 500	0	+		+1,000		0		+600		- 400	
6/1/13 Withdraw all $1,200 from biz checking to pay owners	- 1,200	0	=		0	+		+1,000	- 1,200	-1,200		+600		- 400	

Figure 14

Lesson 8: How to Prepare Financial Statements (Balance Sheet & Income Statement)

In lesson 5 we used our team points analogy to introduce the concept of financial statements—the balance sheet and income statement. After we recorded team points for games 1 and 2, we summarized the points two ways using two reports in Figure 6. We first looked at "Team Points as of 2/1/13," mentioning that it's like a balance sheet. We then looked at "My Points from 1/1/13 – 2/1/13," mentioning that it's like an income statement.

In this lesson, we're doing the same thing for real-world business transactions as of 4/1/13, as shown in Figure 15.

Balance Sheet:

See the bottom-left box in Figure 15 below. We see that the Balance Sheet is summarizing everything we've accounted for *as of* 4/1/13. Total assets show up at the top. Liabilities and owners' equity show up at the bottom. Notice how this just turns the accounting equation 90 degrees. Also notice how this report covers a *point* in time rather than—as the income statement covers—a *period* of time.

Income Statement:

See the bottom-right box in Figure 15 below. We see that the income statement is summarizing only revenues and expenses for the entire period of interest,

1/1/13 through 4/1/13. Notice how this report covers a *period* of time rather than a *point* in time. Also notice how, as we subtract expenses from revenues on the face of the income statement, we calculate net income (also known as profit, or the "bottom line").

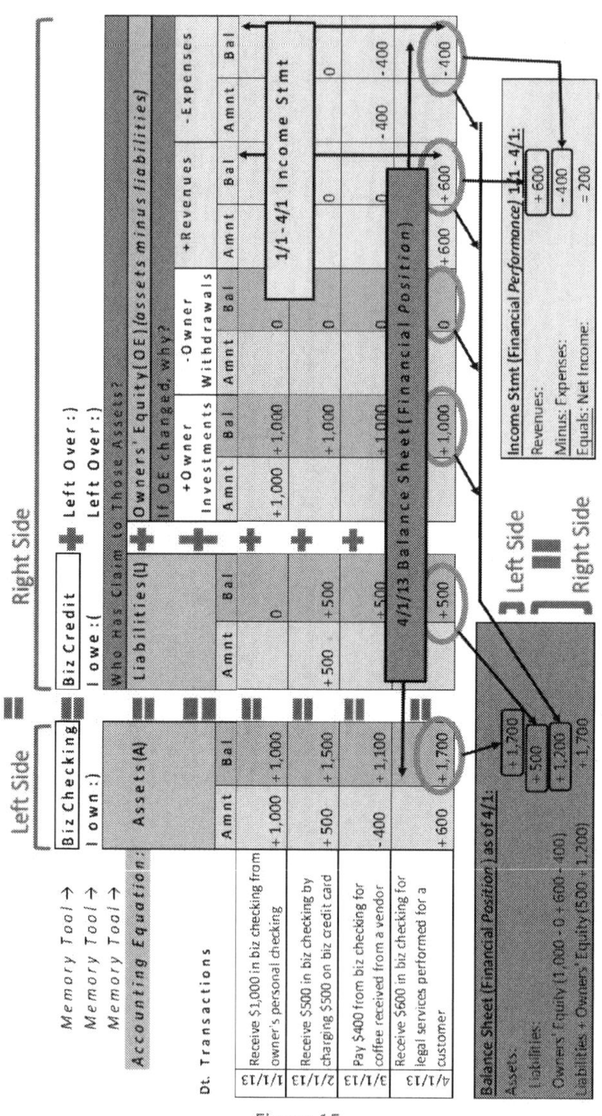
Left Side
Right Side
Memory Tool → Biz Checking = Biz Credit + Left Over :)
Memory Tool → I own :) I owe :(Left Over :)
Memory Tool → Who Has Claim to Those Assets?
Accounting Equation: Assets(A) = Liabilities(L) + Owners' Equity(OE) (assets minus liabilities)
If OE changed, why?
+Owner Investments
-Owner Withdrawals
+Revenues
-Expenses
Dt.
Transactions
Amnt
Bal
1/1/13
Receive $1,000 in biz checking from owner's personal checking
2/1/13
Receive $500 in biz checking by charging $500 on biz credit card
3/1/13
Pay $400 from biz checking for coffee received from a vendor
4/1/13
Receive $600 in biz checking for legal services performed for a customer
1/1-4/1 Income Stmt
4/1/13 Balance Sheet (Financial Position)
Balance Sheet (Financial Position) as of 4/1:
Assets:
Liabilities:
Owners' Equity (1,000 - 0 + 600 - 400)
Liabilities + Owners' Equity (500 + 1,200)
Income Stmt (Financial Performance) 1/1-4/1:
Revenues:
Minus: Expenses:
Equals: Net Income:
Left Side
=
Right Side

Figure 15

Lesson 9: General Ledger Accounts & the Chart of Accounts

Now that we have used the accounting equation to record common transactions and prepare financial statements, we can take a step back to appreciate how the accounting equation captures every kind of account an organization may have. See Figure 16. Regardless of how many asset accounts an organization may have—cash, accounts receivable, inventory, etc.—they will always fall under the "assets" heading of the accounting equation. Likewise, regardless of how many liabilities accounts an organization may have—accounts payable, long-term debt, etc.—they will always fall under the "liabilities" heading of the accounting equation.

You may see section 2 for a more in-depth looks at the types of assets, liabilities, and equity accounts an organization may have.

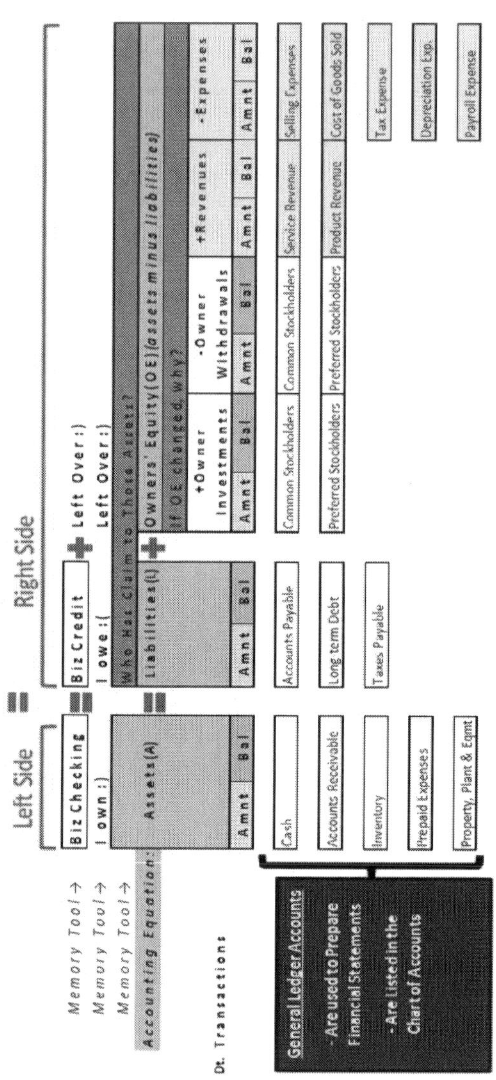
Left Side
Right Side
Memory Tool →
Biz Checking
Biz Credit
Left Over :)
Memory Tool →
I own :)
I owe :(
Left Over :)
Memory Tool →
Accounting Equation:
Assets(A)
Liabilities(L)
Owners' Equity(OE)(assets minus liabilities)
Who Has Claim to Those Assets?
If OE changed why?
+Owner Investments
-Owner Withdrawals
+Revenues
-Expenses
Amnt
Bal
Dr. Transactions
Cash
Accounts Receivable
Inventory
Prepaid Expenses
Property, Plant & Eqmt
Accounts Payable
Long term Debt
Taxes Payable
Common Stockholders
Preferred Stockholders
Common Stockholders
Preferred Stockholders
Service Revenue
Product Revenue
Selling Expenses
Cost of Goods Sold
Tax Expense
Depreciation Exp.
Payroll Expense
General Ledger Accounts
- Are used to Prepare Financial Statements
- Are Listed in the Chart of Accounts

Figure 16

Chapter 4: Debits & Credits

Lessons 2-9 gave us a solid grasp of core accounting topics using plusses and minuses. By lessons 10-13 we're ready to learn how to use debits and credits to record business transactions, rather than plusses and minuses. We see that preparing the financial statements from debits and credits is very easy business. We conclude with a quick reference chart for debits and credits that makes it easy to recall how to use debits and credits to record every type of transaction.

- *Lesson 10: Intro to Debits & Credits*
- *Lesson 11: How to use Debits & Credits to Record Transactions & Prepare Financial Statements (Balance Sheet & Income Statement)*
- *Lesson 12: Debits & Credits – Quick Reference*

Lesson 10: Intro to Debits & Credits

Before we move into learning debits and credits, we can look again at the accounting equation framework we used to record the transactions in Figure 17. Notice the plusses and minuses in this Figure. With each of our transactions, we recorded a positive or a negative number on the left side of the account equation ("assets"), and then a positive or negative number on the right side ("Who has claim to those assets?"). Notice how with every transaction we kept the accounting equation in balance; the left side always equaled the right side.

As we move on to recording transactions using debits and credits, recall that we are essentially doing the same thing we did with plusses and minuses. We are recording each transaction amount twice, once to the left side of the accounting equation and once to its right side *(this means we are using the double-entry accounting method introduced in lesson 3, figure 4)*. We are recording each transaction amount to the appropriate accounts using the accounting equation, always keeping the accounting equation's left and right sides in balance.

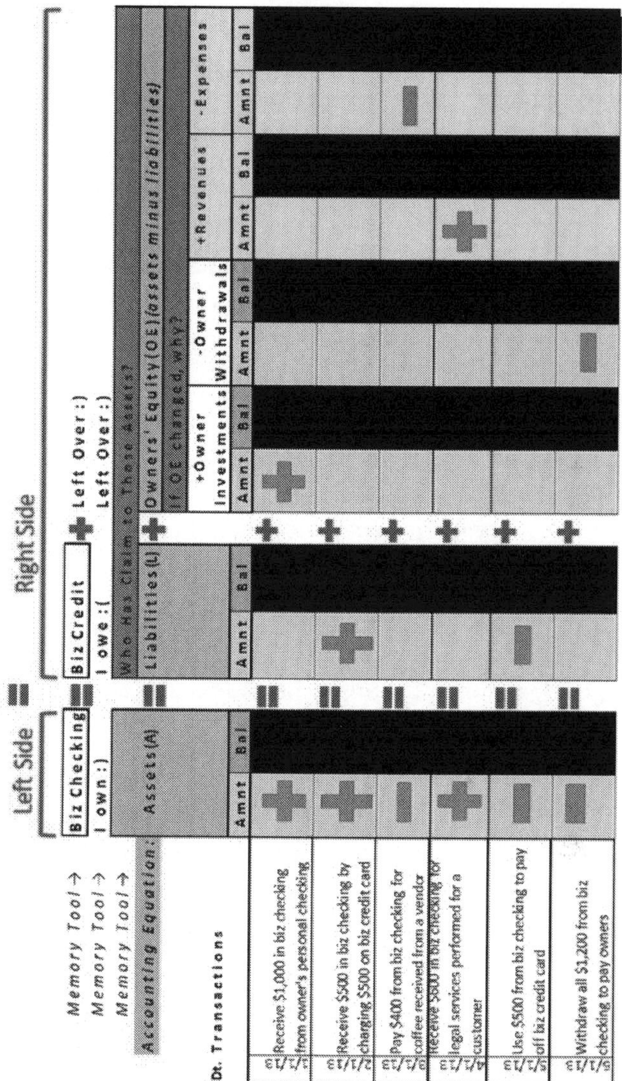
Left Side
=
Right Side
Memory Tool →
Biz Checking
=
Biz Credit
+
Left Over :)
Memory Tool →
I own :)
I owe :(
Left Over :)
Memory Tool →
Accounting Equation:
Assets(A)
=
Who Has Claim to These Assets?
Liabilities(L)
+
Owners' Equity(OE)(assets minus liabilities)
If OE changed, why?
+Owner Investments
-Owner Withdrawals
+Revenues
-Expenses
Amnt
Bal
Dt.
Transactions
1/1/13
Receive $1,000 in biz checking from owner's personal checking
2/1/13
Receive $500 in biz checking by charging $500 on biz credit card
3/1/13
Pay $400 from biz checking for coffee received from a vendor
4/1/13
Receive $600 in biz checking for legal services performed for a customer
5/1/13
Use $500 from biz checking to pay off biz credit card
6/1/13
Withdraw all $1,200 from biz checking to pay owners

Figure 17

Lesson 11: How to use Debits & Credits to Record Transactions & Prepare Financial Statements (Balance Sheet & Income Statement)

We can say that rule #1 of debits and credits is that debit means left-side and credit means right-side. (Do not think of debit as good or bad. Do not think of credit as good or bad.) When we visualize debits and credits for a particular account, such as the asset account cash, we use something called a T-account, or a T-chart. See Figure 18. We put the account title on the top, "Cash" for example. *All* debit amounts go on the left side, and *all* credit amounts go on the right side.

What we will see in the following transaction examples is that for some accounts we use debits to increase the account's balance (*and credits to decrease the accounts' balance*). For other accounts we use credits to increase the account's balance (*and debits to decrease the accounts' balance*).

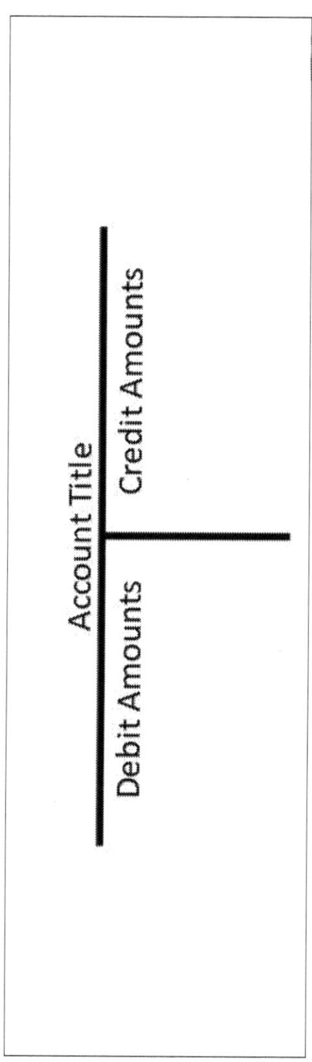

Figure 18

We can say that rule #2 of debits and credits is that, for any particular transaction, the debits *have to* equal the credits. See Figure 19.

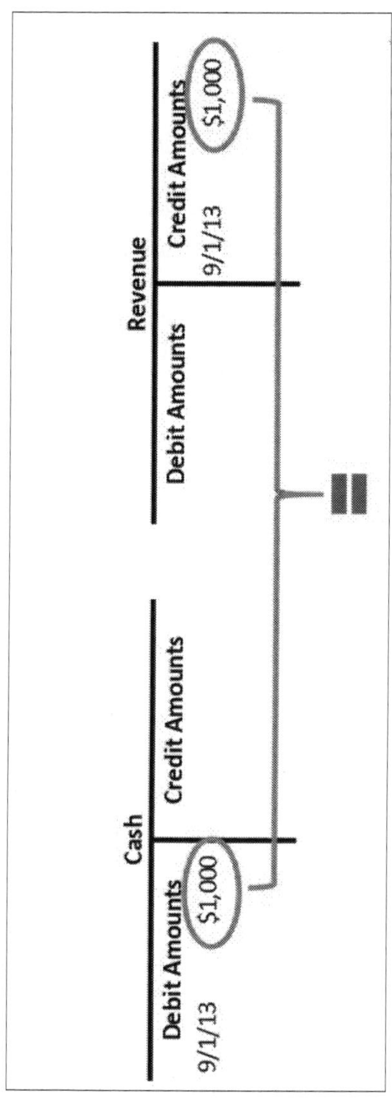
Cash
Debit Amounts
Credit Amounts
9/1/13
$1,000
Revenue
Debit Amounts
Credit Amounts
9/1/13
$1,000

Figure 19

See Figure 20. We can say that rule #3 of debits and credits is that you *must* debit *asset* accounts to *increase* them (and credit asset accounts to decrease them). With a little practice, you will soon memorize this rule. Luckily, it is one of only a few rules for using debits and credits.

See Figure 21 to see how debits and credits in T-accounts are used to record transactions to any account. Notice that plusses and minuses are not used, but rather left-side entries (debits) and right-side entries (credits).

Also notice in Figure 21 how the running balance at any point in time is just as easy to calculate as it was with the plusses-and-minuses method. Instead of having a positive or negative balance at any point in time, the account is said to have either a debit balance or credit balance.

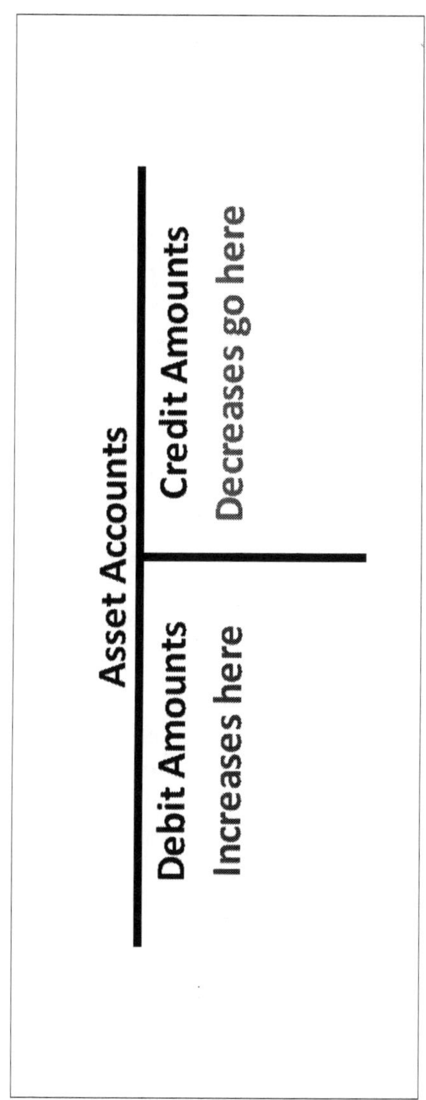
Asset Accounts
Debit Amounts
Increases here
Credit Amounts
Decreases go here

Figure 20

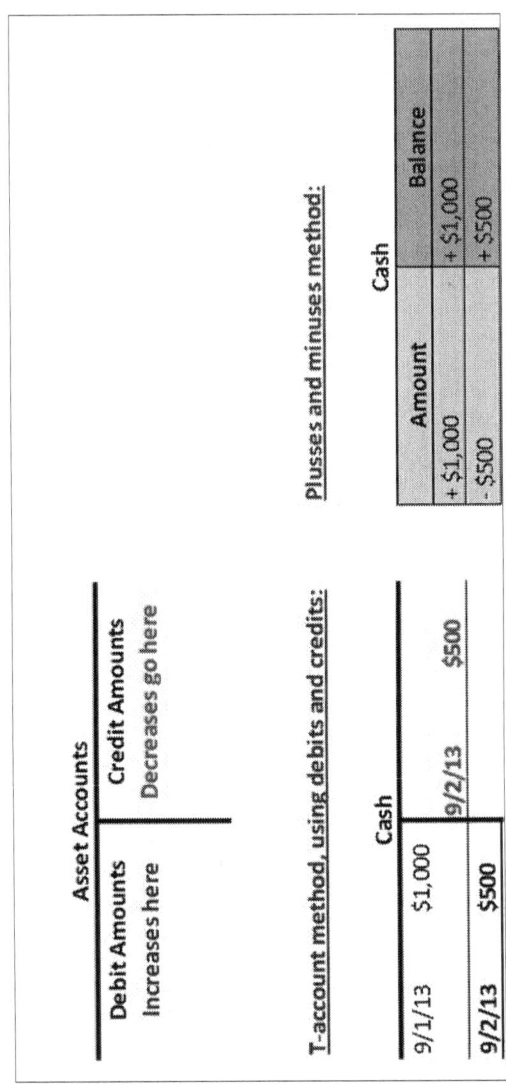
Asset Accounts
Debit Amounts
Increases here
Credit Amounts
Decreases go here
T-account method, using debits and credits:
Cash
9/1/13 $1,000
9/2/13 $500
9/2/13 $500
Plusses and minuses method:
Cash
Amount
Balance
+ $1,000
+ $1,000
- $500
+ $500

Figure 21

Figures 22 through 25 show how debits and credits are used to record the same transactions we recorded in the previous lesson using plusses and minuses.

Notice how, just as we did in the previous lesson with the plusses-and-minuses method, we start with the left side of the accounting equation and ask, "What happened to total assets?" We know that rule #3 of debits and credits says we must *debit* asset accounts to *increase* them (and credit asset accounts to decrease them). So, if the asset account cash went *up*, we *debited* the account. If the cash account went *down*, we *credited* the account.

Also notice how, just as we did in the previous lesson with the plusses-and-minuses method, we look to the right side of the accounting equation and ask, "Who has claim to those assets?" We know that rule #2 of debits and credits is that, for any particular transaction, the debits *have to* equal the credits. So, if we debited the cash account (on the left side of the accounting equation), we credited the other account involved in the transaction (on the right side of the accounting equation).

Figure 26 shows us how the debit or credit account balances as of 4/1/13 are used to prepare the balance sheet and the income statement, just as we did in the previous lesson using plusses and minuses.

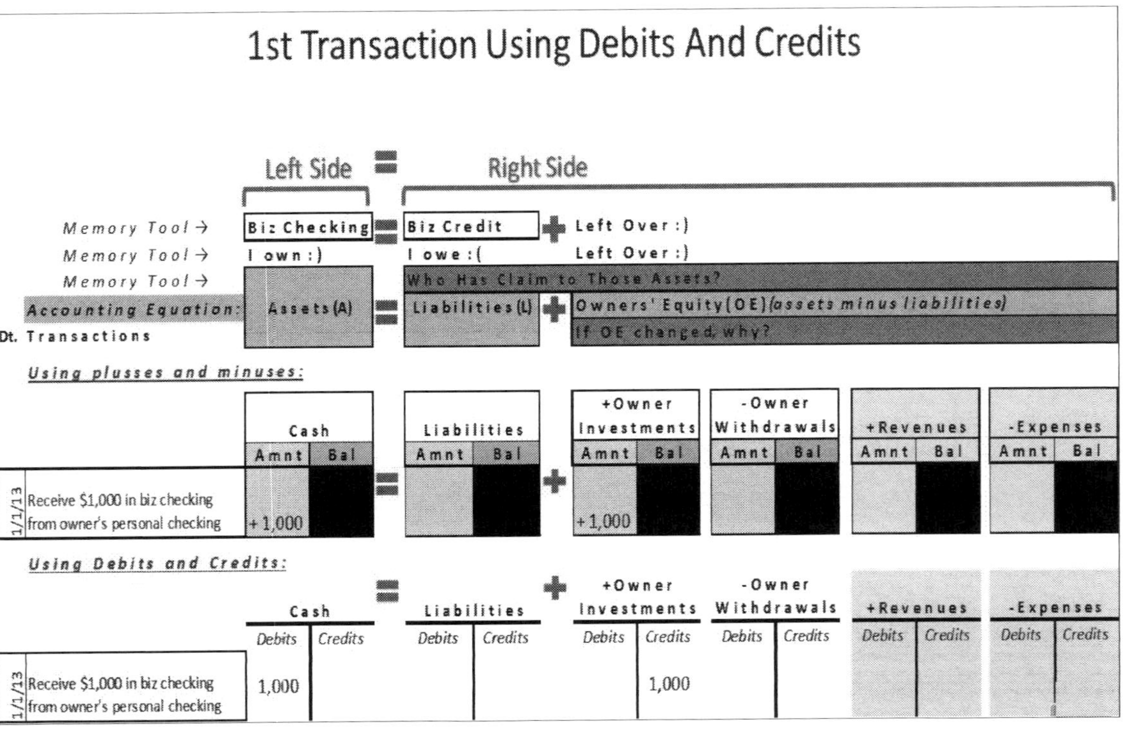
1st Transaction Using Debits And Credits
Left Side
Right Side
Memory Tool →
Biz Checking
Biz Credit
Left Over :)
Memory Tool →
I own :)
I owe :(
Left Over :)
Memory Tool →
Who Has Claim to Those Assets?
Accounting Equation:
Assets (A)
Liabilities (L)
Owners' Equity (OE) (assets minus liabilities)
If OE changed, why?
Dt. Transactions
Using plusses and minuses:
Cash
Amnt
Bal
Liabilities
Amnt
Bal
+Owner Investments
Amnt
Bal
-Owner Withdrawals
Amnt
Bal
+Revenues
Amnt
Bal
-Expenses
Amnt
Bal
1/1/13 Receive $1,000 in biz checking from owner's personal checking
+ 1,000
+ 1,000
Using Debits and Credits:
Cash
Debits
Credits
Liabilities
Debits
Credits
+Owner Investments
Debits
Credits
-Owner Withdrawals
Debits
Credits
+Revenues
Debits
Credits
-Expenses
Debits
Credits
1/1/13 Receive $1,000 in biz checking from owner's personal checking
1,000
1,000

Figure 22

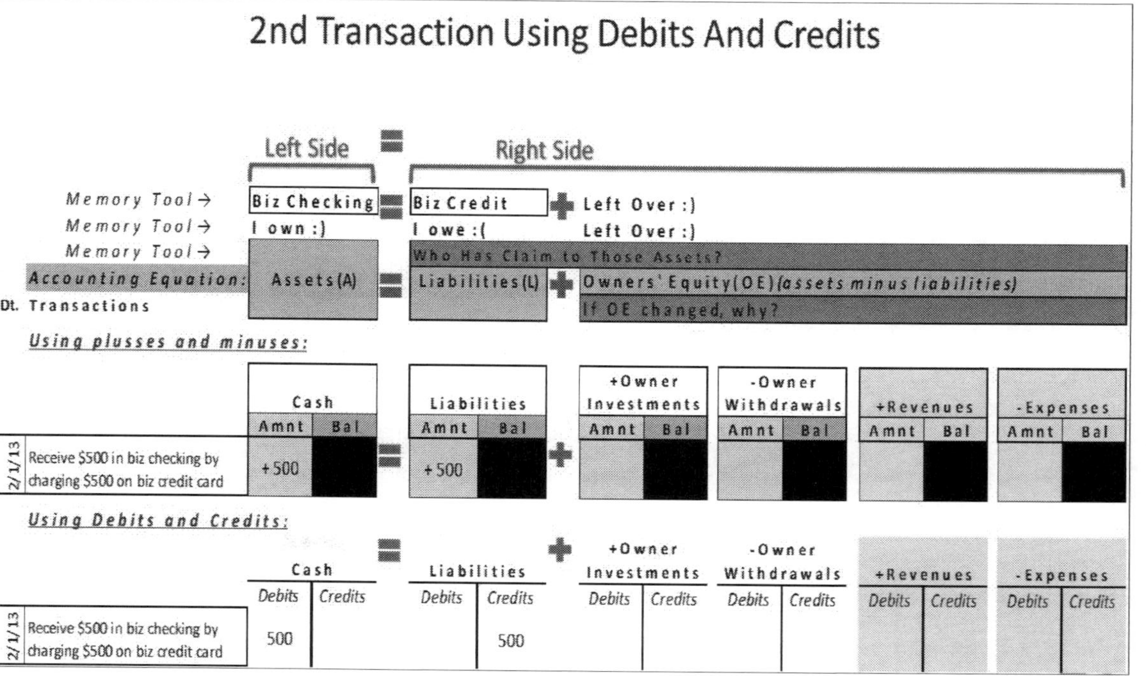
2nd Transaction Using Debits And Credits
Left Side
=
Right Side
Memory Tool →
Biz Checking
=
Biz Credit
+
Left Over :)
Memory Tool →
I own :)
I owe :(
Left Over :)
Memory Tool →
Who Has Claim to Those Assets?
Accounting Equation:
Assets(A)
=
Liabilities(L)
+
Owners' Equity(OE)(assets minus liabilities)
Dt.
Transactions
If OE changed, why?
Using plusses and minuses:
Cash
Amnt
Bal
Liabilities
Amnt
Bal
+Owner Investments
Amnt
Bal
-Owner Withdrawals
Amnt
Bal
+Revenues
Amnt
Bal
-Expenses
Amnt
Bal
2/1/13
Receive $500 in biz checking by charging $500 on biz credit card
+500
+500
Using Debits and Credits:
Cash
Debits
Credits
Liabilities
Debits
Credits
+Owner Investments
Debits
Credits
-Owner Withdrawals
Debits
Credits
+Revenues
Debits
Credits
-Expenses
Debits
Credits
2/1/13
Receive $500 in biz checking by charging $500 on biz credit card
500
500

Figure 23

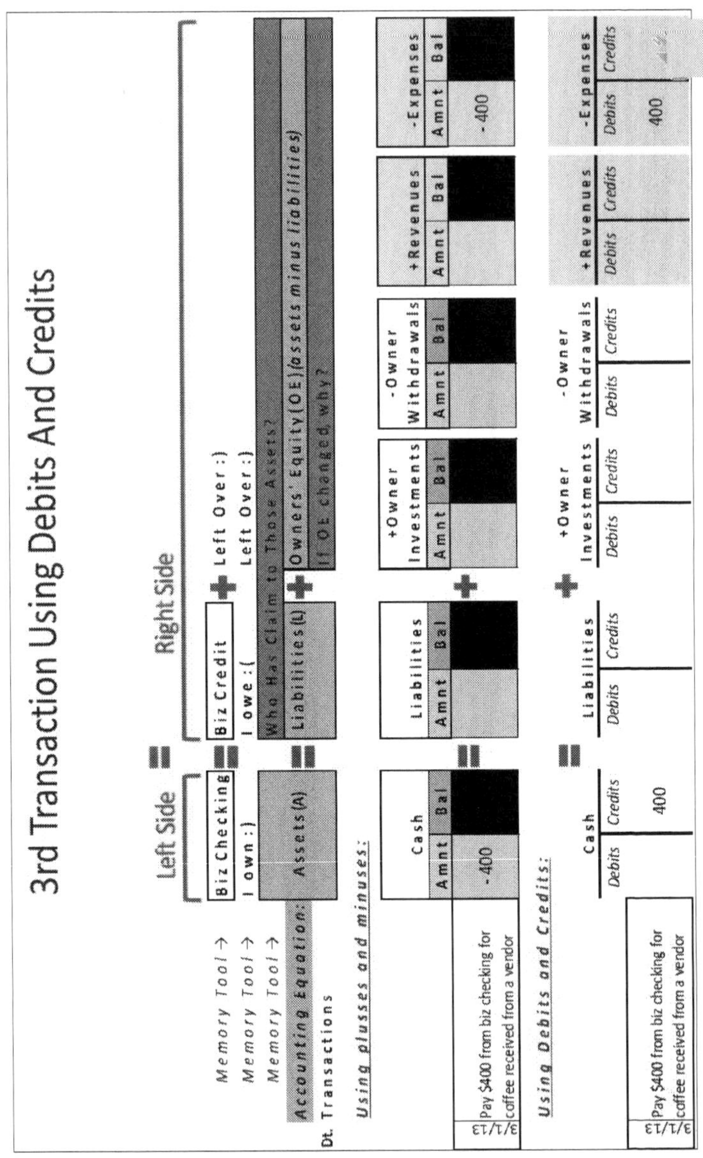
3rd Transaction Using Debits And Credits
Left Side
Right Side
Memory Tool →
Biz Checking
Biz Credit
Left Over :)
Memory Tool →
I own :)
I owe :(
Left Over :)
Memory Tool →
Who Has Claim to Those Assets?
Accounting Equation:
Assets(A)
Liabilities(L)
Owners' Equity(OE)(assets minus liabilities)
If OE changed, why?
Dt.
Transactions
Using plusses and minuses:
Cash
Amnt
Bal
-400
Liabilities
Amnt
Bal
+Owner Investments
Amnt
Bal
-Owner Withdrawals
Amnt
Bal
+Revenues
Amnt
Bal
-Expenses
Amnt
Bal
-400
3/1/13
Pay $400 from biz checking for coffee received from a vendor
Using Debits and Credits:
Cash
Debits
Credits
400
Liabilities
Debits
Credits
+Owner Investments
Debits
Credits
-Owner Withdrawals
Debits
Credits
+Revenues
Debits
Credits
-Expenses
Debits
Credits
400
3/1/13
Pay $400 from biz checking for coffee received from a vendor

Figure 24

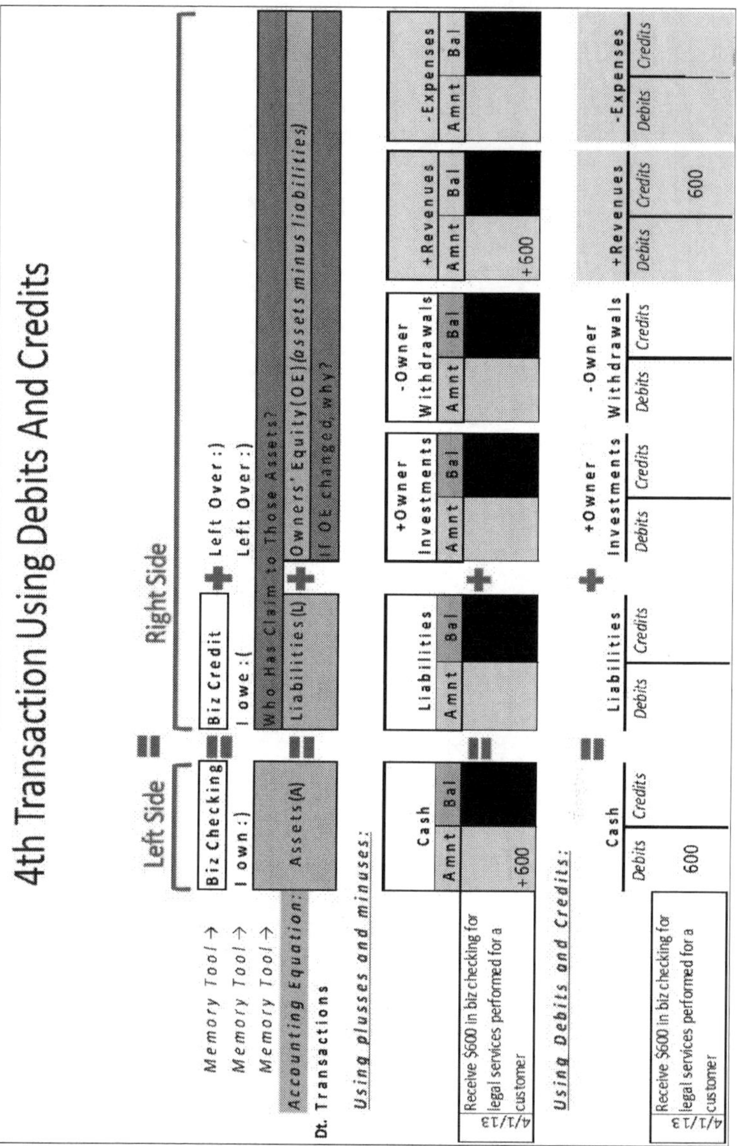
4th Transaction Using Debits And Credits
Left Side
Right Side
Memory Tool →
Biz Checking
Biz Credit
Left Over :)
Memory Tool →
I own :)
I owe :(
Left Over :)
Memory Tool →
Who Has Claim to Those Assets?
Accounting Equation:
Assets(A)
Liabilities(L)
Owners' Equity(OE)(assets minus liabilities)
Dt. Transactions
If OE changed, why?
Using plusses and minuses:
Cash
Liabilities
+Owner Investments
-Owner Withdrawals
+Revenues
-Expenses
Amnt
Bal
4/1/13
Receive $600 in biz checking for legal services performed for a customer
+600
+600
Using Debits and Credits:
Cash
Liabilities
+Owner Investments
-Owner Withdrawals
+Revenues
-Expenses
Debits
Credits
4/1/13
Receive $600 in biz checking for legal services performed for a customer
600
600

Figure 25

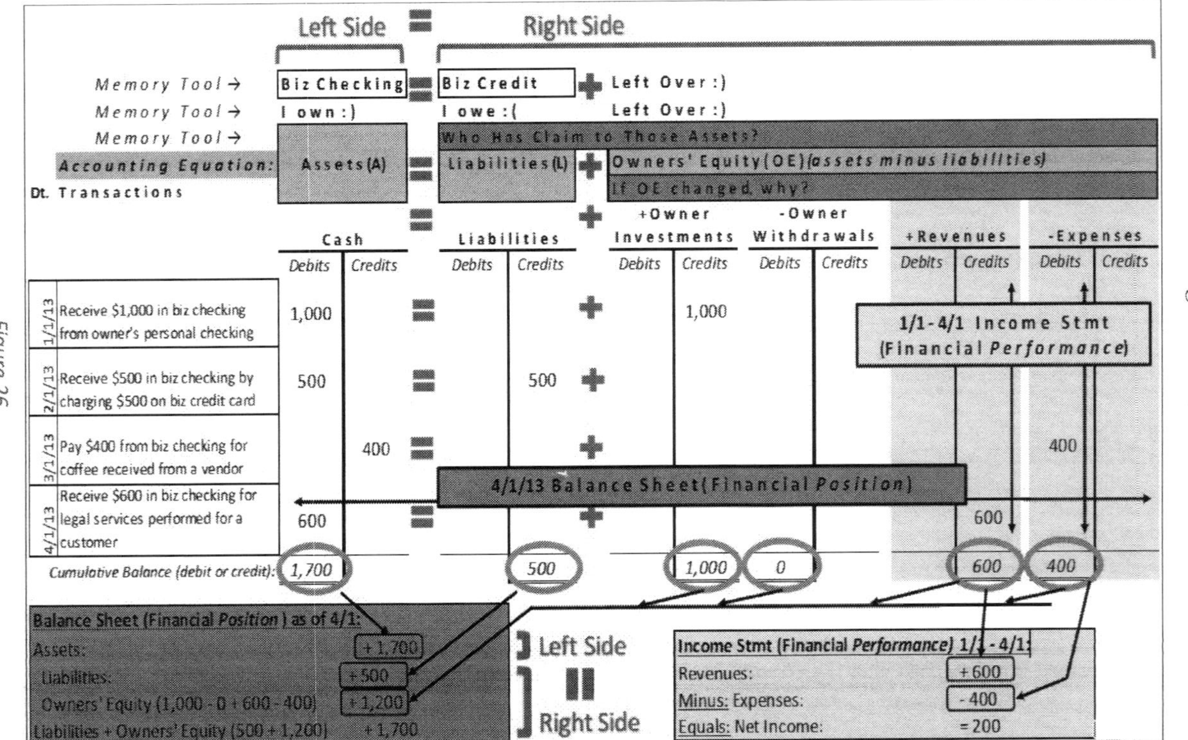
Left Side
=
Right Side
Memory Tool →
Biz Checking
=
Biz Credit
+
Left Over :)
Memory Tool →
I own :)
I owe :(
Left Over :)
Memory Tool →
Who Has Claim to Those Assets?
Accounting Equation:
Assets(A)
=
Liabilities(L)
+
Owners' Equity(OE)(assets minus liabilities)
If OE changed, why?
Dt.
Transactions
Cash
Liabilities
+Owner Investments
-Owner Withdrawals
+Revenues
-Expenses
Debits
Credits
1/1/13
Receive $1,000 in biz checking from owner's personal checking
1,000
1,000
2/1/13
Receive $500 in biz checking by charging $500 on biz credit card
500
500
3/1/13
Pay $400 from biz checking for coffee received from a vendor
400
400
4/1/13
Receive $600 in biz checking for legal services performed for a customer
600
600
Cumulative Balance (debit or credit):
1,700
500
1,000
0
600
400
1/1-4/1 Income Stmt (Financial Performance)
4/1/13 Balance Sheet (Financial Position)
Balance Sheet (Financial Position) as of 4/1:
Assets:
+ 1,700
Liabilities:
+500
Owners' Equity (1,000 - 0 + 600 - 400)
+1,200
Liabilities + Owners' Equity (500 + 1,200)
+ 1,700
Left Side
=
Right Side
Income Stmt (Financial Performance) 1/1 - 4/1:
Revenues:
+600
Minus: Expenses:
-400
Equals: Net Income:
= 200

Figure 26

Debits & Credits – Quick Reference

These accounts are **increased** with **debits:**	These accounts are **increased** with **credits:**
Dividends *	Gains
Expenses	Income
Assets	Revenues
Losses	Liabilities
	Stockholders' Equity **

** Dividends are like "Owner Withdrawals" in our examples. This account records payments from the organization to its owner(s).*

*** Stockholders' Equity is like "Owners' Equity" in our examples, the amount on the balance sheet that is left over after liabilities are subtracted from assets.*

- Losses are like expenses in that they decrease net income on the income statement.

- Gains & Income are like Revenue in that they increase net income on the income statement.

Figure 27

SECTION 2: A CLOSER LOOK

Section 2 takes a closer look at basic accounting. It covers much of the same concepts covered in section 1 in greater depth. For example, in Section 1 you learn how transactions are first recorded in journal entries and later summarized in financial statements, like the balance sheet and income statement. Section 2 expands on this by showing the “middle step” between the initial journal entry recording and the financial statements: the trial balance. Trial balance is just a fancy term for a list of account balances at a point in time—it’ll be an easy learn by the time we get here.

Section 2 introduces new concepts such as accrual accounting, where we adjust revenues and expenses for transactions where cash isn’t going in or out the door at the same time. We learn the third and fourth of the four major financial statements (statement of retained earnings and statement of cash flows). Again, no need to worry. By the time we get there these items will make perfect sense.

Chapter 5: Building Blocks of Financial Statements

Transaction Analysis

- Transaction
- Account
- Record
- Journal

Double-Entry Accounting

Accounting Equation

Ledger, General Ledger, Chart of Accounts, & Trial Balance

- Ledger
- Posting
- General ledger
- Trial balance (TB)
    - Unadjusted trial balance (TB)
    - Adjusted trial balance (TB)

Debits & Credits

- T-Accounts

Transaction Analysis. Transaction analysis means taking a narrative of what happened in a transaction *(e.g. ABC Company performed a service to a customer for $100)*, determining which accounts are affected by the transaction (e.g., assets and revenue), determining whether each account increased or decreased (e.g. assets increase and revenue increased), determining whether each account must be debited or credited (e.g. debit assets, credit revenues), and recording the transaction in the accounting system (i.e. making the debit/credit entry in a journal).

- Transaction. A financial exchange (e.g. a sale to a customer, where the customer exchanges money, or a promise to pay, for a good or service.)
- Account. A category of a financial item the company needs to track, such as assets, liabilities, revenue, and expenses. For example, the company may have an asset account for its buildings. Changes to account balances are tracked using entries in journals. *(It may be helpful to think of an account as a bucket. Your bank statement is a great example of an asset account.)*
- Record (AKA journalize, or enter) (when used as a *verb*). Entering a transaction in a journal. This means the transaction has been introduced into the accounting system, and will affect the financial statements. The journalized transaction is known as an entry, or journal entry.
- Journal. A record of transactions in debit/credit format. Debit/credit entries made into the journals are transferred to the general ledger, which is used to prepare the trial balance, which is used to prepare the financial statements. A company may have multiple journals, for example a sales journal, disbursements journal, payroll journal, and so on. A company may also

have a "general journal," to keep track of transactions that don't belong in specific journals, such as non-routine transactions.

- Note: Journals are used *in practice* instead of T-accounts because using T-accounts would be too difficult. However, T-accounts are helpful visual aids when learning accounting, as shown below.

Journal Entry:

Date	Account Name	Debit	Credit
1/1/11	Supplies Expense	$100	
	Cash		$100

Double-Entry Accounting. Accounting procedure of recording every transactions with two or more accounts. For each transaction, the debits equal the credits, and the accounting equation Assets (A) = Liabilities (L) + Owners' Equity (OE) is kept in balance.

Note: Stated another way, double-entry accounting means using multiple account entries to keep track of one event from multiple perspectives. If the business were only interested in the running total of its assets, it could use one entry per transaction to record changes to the asset accounts, such as cash, vehicles, buildings, etc. In this hypothetical case, only the "A" side of the accounting equation A = L + OE would be needed. However, the business needs to track not only the changes to assets, but also the *reason why* those changes occurred. Some asset increases were due to owners investing in the business, while other asset increases were due to paying customers. If a business needs to calculate total profit at yearend, it will need separate accounts to track transactions with its owners, and other accounts to track transactions with its customers (revenue accounts) and suppliers (expense accounts). This way, at the end of the year the business can add up the revenue transactions, add up the expense transactions, and subtract total expenses from total revenues to arrive at total net income, or profit.

Accounting Equation. Equation showing how assets equal liabilities plus owners' equity (A = L + OE). The equation can be rearranged to A – L = OE, although this is not formally called the accounting equation.

Note: The left side equals the right side in the accounting equation, because each side records the same events, just from different perspectives. See Double-Entry Accounting above for more clarification.

Ledgers, General Ledger, Chart of Accounts, & Trial Balance.

- A ledger is a chronological record of changes to one specific account balance over time, and the running account balance after each transaction.

Ledger Example:

Cash				
Date	Description	Debit	Credit	Balance
	Beginning Balance			$500
1/1/11	Paid for Supplies Expense		$100	$400

- Posting. Copying debit/credit information from a journal to the general ledger. *(Note: Information copied for each account includes the transaction date, and debit and credit amounts.)*
    - Note that journals show only a record of transactions in debit/credit form, and the multiple accounts affected. Journals don't show a running balance and are not prepared for just one account.

Journal Entry:

Date	Account Name	Debit	Credit
1/1/11	Supplies Expense Cash	$100	 $100

Ledger Example:

Cash				
Date	Description	Debit	Credit	Balance
	Beginning Balance			$500
1/1/11	Paid for Supplies Expense		$100	$400

- The general ledger is the group of ledgers for all of the company's accounts (e.g. asset accounts, liability accounts, etc.). These accounts are also called general ledger accounts, indicating that they are a part of the general ledger. The account balances of general ledger accounts are used to prepare the trial balance, which is used to prepare the financial statements.
- The general ledger accounts are listed in the Chart of Accounts, which is simply a list of general ledger accounts (e.g. a Bake Shop's Chart of Accounts may list 34 accounts, including a "sugar supplies" expense account, and may identify next to each account name a unique account number.
- Trial balance (TB). List of all accounts and their balances (either debit or credit) as of a certain date. The purpose of the trial balance (TB) is to verify that total debits equal total credits.
  - For example, all cash accounts on the TB might have an "11" at the beginning of the account number. Perhaps cash account 112 records transactions of a Wells Fargo bank account and cash account 113 records transactions of a Discover account used for payroll. The business might add all account balances from the TB that start with "11" and put the total as "Cash" on the balance sheet.
  - Account balances from the general ledger are used to prepare the unadjusted TB, adjusted TB, and post-closing TB.

- *Unadjusted* trial balance (TB): A TB prepared at the end of the accounting period ***before*** adjusting entries are made. (Adjusting entries are discussed in chapter 6.)
- *Adjusted* trial balance (TB): A TB prepared at the end of the accounting period ***after*** adjusting entries are made.
    - The *adjusted* TB is used to prepare the financial statements.

ABC Company
Trial Balance (Adjusted; Before Closing Entries)
12/31/2013

Account Title	Balance	
	Debit	Credit
Assets:		
Cash	$XX	
Accounts receivable	$XX	
Prepaid expenses	$XX	
Vehicles	$XX	
Buildings	$XX	
Equipment	$XX	
Liabilities:		
Accounts payable		$XX
Credit Card		$XX
Unearned Revenue		$XX
Equity:		
Common stock		$XX
Dividends		$XX

Retained earnings		$XX
Service Revenue		$XX
Goods Revenue		$XX
Service Expenses	$XX	
Cost of Goods Sold	$XX	
Total	$XXX	$XXX

Debit and Credits. See Figure 28 below. Debit means left-side of an account, credit means right-side of an account. (Do not think of debit as good or bad. Do not think of credit as good or bad.) Each entry's debit amount must equal the credit amount.

Technical Note: By using debits to increase certain account types and credits to increase other account types, the accounting equation A = L + SE is *automatically* kept in balance. If instead of debits and credits we used plusses and minuses to keep track of accounts, we could *accidentally* cause the accounting equation to come out of balance by recording a transactions with an incorrect sign. For example, when we paid cash for an expense, the expense account should “go up” because there are more expenses. However, we could accidentally decrease (use a minus sign), when a plus sign was needed for the expense account. This possibility for human error is removed when we assign debit-credit rules that say the asset, dividends, and expenses account types are increased with debits (left-side entries) while the liability, common stock, and revenue account types are increased with credits (right-side entries). For our example, these rules that apply are: debits (left-side entries) are always used to increase asset accounts and debits (right-side entries) are always used to increase expense accounts. We paid cash, so the asset account cash decreased and therefore we credited the account (right-side entry). The expense account increased, so we debited the account (left-side entry). If we accidentally recorded a credit to the expense account instead of a debit, the debits would not equal the credits for the transaction, and our accounting software would easily show us that (*or if we were using a paper system we would easily see this mistake when checking for equality between the debits and credits of the entry*).

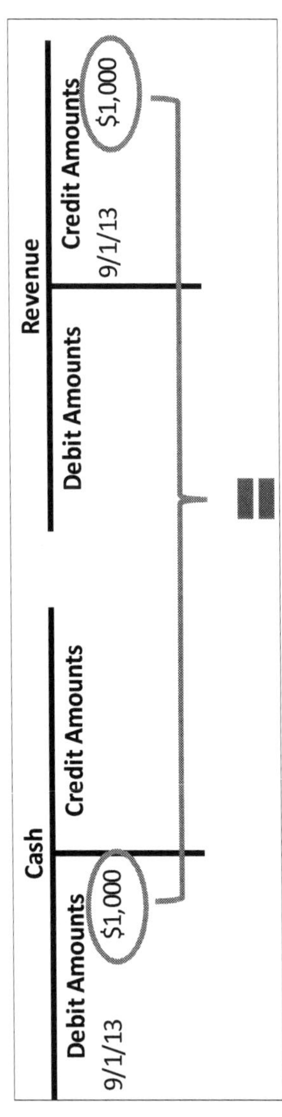
Cash
Debit Amounts
Credit Amounts
9/1/13
$1,000
Revenue
Debit Amounts
Credit Amounts
9/1/13
$1,000

Figure 28

T-Account. See Figure 29 below. A visual aid in the shape of a T which uses a vertical line to separate the debits (left-side entries) and credits (right-side entries) to an account. A T-account can be drawn for any account, such as cash, buildings, etc. The account title is placed at the top of the T. T-accounts are used as visual aids to learn accounting and also to show how transactions affect multiple accounts. However, T-accounts are not *formally* a part of an accounting information system (i.e. software.) They are *not* a part of journals, ledgers, trial balances, or financial statements.

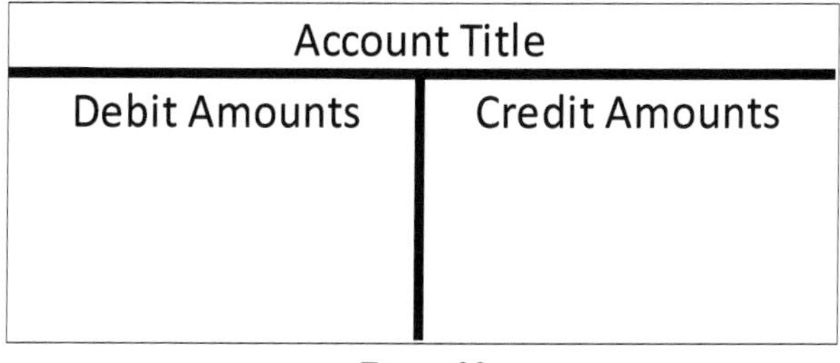

Figure 29

Chapter 6: Accrual Accounting

Accrual accounting

- Revenue recognition principle
- Matching Principle
- Accruals
- Deferrals
- Adjusting Entries
    - Accrual adjustments
        - Record Accrued Revenues
        - Record Accrued Expenses
    - Deferral adjustments.
        - Adjust Deferred Revenues
        - Adjust Deferred Expenses
            - Depreciation

Accrual accounting means recording revenues when *earned* and expenses when *incurred*, ***regardless*** of when cash is exchanged. Accrual accounting means following the revenue recognition principle and the matching principle, and is carried out using accruals, deferrals and adjusting entries, all covered in this chapter.

Revenue recognition principle. Record (i.e. recognize) revenues *when they are earned*, ***regardless*** of when cash is received.

Matching Principle. The Matching Principle says to record expenses in the period they are *incurred*, ***regardless*** of when cash is paid. An expense being "incurred" essentially means *used* to generate revenue. Therefore, the Matching Principle matches expenses to the revenues they helped generate; the revenue and matched expense are recorded in the same period, so that the period's net income (revenues minus expenses) gives an accurate picture of profit earned.

Example of Revenue Recognition Principle and Matching Principle. You bought a widget in January, sold the widget to a customer in February, and got paid by the customer in March. The revenue recognition principle says that revenue must be recorded in February, as this was the month revenue was *earned*. The matching principle says you must record the expense in the period of the revenue the expense helped generate, so February in our example. This way, if you were to print an income statement covering February only, you would see both the revenue and expense (if you received revenue of $1 and the widget cost you $0.90, profit would be $0.10 for February on the income statement). If you waited until March to record the revenue, February's income statement would show expense with no related revenue (a loss equals to the $0.90 expense), and March's income statement would show revenue with no related expense (so profit equal to the $1 of revenue).

Accruals. An Accrual is a recording of *revenue earned before cash receipt ("Accrued Revenue")*, or expense incurred *before cash payment ("Accrued Expense").*

Accrued Revenue example: Record revenue for widget sold in February, even though cash will not be collected from the customer until March.

Journal Entry:

Date	Account Name	Debit	Credit
2/28/11	Accounts Receivable	$50	
	Revenue		$50
3/30/11	Cash	$50	
	Accounts Receivable		$50

Accrued Expense example: Record utilities expense for electricity used in September, even though you will not pay the utility bill until October.

Journal Entry:

Date	Account Name	Debit	Credit
9/30/11	Utilities Expense	$560	
	Accounts Payable		$560
10/31/11	Accounts Payable	$560	
	Cash		$560

Deferrals. A Deferral is a recording of a *cash receipt before the revenue is earned ("Deferred Revenue")*, or *cash payment before the expense is incurred ("Deferred Expense")*. Note that in general, when cash receipt is recorded prior to revenue being earned, a corresponding liability is also recorded, and when cash payment is recorded prior to the expense being incurred, a corresponding asset is also recorded.)

Deferred revenue example: You receive cash from a customer in January for services you perform for the customer in February. In January, along with recording the increase in cash, you record a liability to the customer in a liability account called "unearned revenue." In February, when you perform the service (i.e. ***earn*** the revenue), you record revenue. Because you no longer owe the customer services in February, you remove the "unearned revenue" liability balance which was recorded in January.

Journal Entry:

Date	Account Name	Debit	Credit
1/31/11	Cash	$160	
	Unearned Revenue		$160
2/28/11	Unearned Revenue	$160	
	Revenue		$160

Deferred expense example: You purchase office supplies in January that are used in February. In January, along with recording the decrease in cash, you record the cost of office supplies to a "prepaid expenses" account (an asset account). In February, when the office supplies are *used* (i.e. you ***incur*** the expense), record office supplies expense (an expense account). Because the supplies have been used they are no longer an asset in February, so you also remove the "prepaid expenses" asset account balance which was recorded in January.

Journal Entry:

Date	Account Name	Debit	Credit
1/31/11	Prepaid Expenses Cash	$260	 $260
2/28/11	Supplies Expense Prepaid Expenses	$260	 $260

Adjusting Entries. Journal entries made *at the end of an accounting period* that adjust account balances as necessary to ensure all revenues earned and expenses incurred have been recorded in accord with accrual accounting, rather than cash accounting. In other words, adjusting the books so that all revenues earned have been recorded, ***regardless*** of when cash has been (or will be) exchanged, and all expenses incurred have been recorded, ***regardless*** of when cash has been (or will be) exchanged. There are four main types of adjusting entries:

Accrual adjustments:

Record Accrued Revenues. Record (or "accrue") any unrecorded revenues. This means revenue that has been *earned*, but cash has not been collected yet. If such revenue *has not already been* recorded at the end of the accounting period, make an adjusting entry to record the revenue (credit a revenue account). Also record an IOU from the party who owes the business (e.g. a customer) in an asset account called "accounts receivable," or "A/R" (debit an A/R account).

Record Accrued Expenses. Record (or "accrue") any unrecorded expenses. This means expenses that have been *incurred*, but cash has not been paid yet. If such expenses *have not already been recorded* at the end of the accounting period, make an adjusting entry to record the expense (debit an expense account). Also record an IOU to the party the business owes (e.g. a supplier) in a liability account called "accounts payable," or "A/P" (credit an A/P account).

Deferral adjustments:

Adjust Deferred Revenues. Adjust deferred revenue (or unearned revenue) for any of such revenue that has now been *earned*. For example. You receive cash from a customer in January for services you perform for the customer in February. In January, along with recording the increase in cash, you record a liability to the customer in a liability account called "unearned revenue." In February, when you perform the service (i.e. *earn* the revenue), you record revenue. Because you no longer owe the customer services in February, you remove the "unearned revenue" liability balance which was recorded in January. The entries in *February* in this example are the adjusting entries.

Adjust Deferred Expenses. Adjust deferred expenses for any of such expenses that have now been *incurred*. For example. You purchase office supplies in January that are used in February. In January, along with recording the decrease in cash, you record the cost of office supplies to a "prepaid expenses" account (an asset account). In February, when the office supplies are *used* (i.e. you *incur* the expense), record office supplies expense (an expense account). Because the supplies have been used they are no longer an asset in February, so you also remove the "prepaid expenses" asset account balance which was recorded in January. The entries in *February* in this example are the adjusting entries.

Depreciation. Depreciation means the expensing (or allocating) of a long-term asset's cost over its useful life, as the asset is "used up." *(Examples: Buildings, equipment, etc. Note that land is not depreciated).* The adjusting entry for depreciation is like the adjustment for "used up" prepaid expenses discussed above, except that the asset being used up lasts longer than a year. In the following example, we are depreciating one-tenth of the building's original cost. Another unique aspect of depreciation expense is that journal entry (5/31/11 in our example) does not credit the asset account *itself* ("Building"). Rather, the credited account is "Accumulated Depreciation—Building." This account keeps track of cumulative depreciation over the life of the asset, and when the balance sheet is prepared the balance in the "Accumulated Depreciation—Building" account will be deducted from the $10,000 original cost in the "Building" account to arrive at the "net" amount for the building.

Journal Entry:

Date	Account Name	Debit	Credit
4/30/11	Building	$10,000	
	Cash		$10,000
5/31/11	Depreciation Expense	$260	
	Accum. Depr.-Bldg		$260

Chapter 6 Summary: Accrual Accounting

	Now (e.g. Jan)	Later (e.g. Feb)
Accrued Revenue	Revenue is recorded	Cash is received
Accrued Expense	Expense is recorded	Cash is paid
Deferred Revenue	Cash is received	Revenue is recorded
Deferred Expense	Cash is paid	Expense is recorded
~ Easy way to remember accruals and deferrals: **Cash later with accruals; Cash now with deferrals.** ~		

Figure 30

Chapter 7: Financial Statements

- Income Statement
- Statement of Retained Earnings
- Balance Sheet
- Statement of Cash Flows

Income statement. A financial statement showing financial *performance (not "position)*. In other words, revenues, expenses and net income over a period of time.

- Revenue. Sales of goods and services to customers.
- Expenses. Use of goods and services from vendors.
- Interest. Expense of using borrowed money.
- Net income (also known as profit). Revenues minus expenses.

Visual of income statement in next section

Statement of Retained Earnings (RE). A financial statement showing beginning retained earnings, changes during given period, and ending RE. Changes to retained earnings during a period arise from net income (this adds to retained earnings) and dividends (this deducts from retained earnings.)

- Net income (also known as profit). Revenues minus expenses.

- Dividends. Payments to owners (note: a good way to think of dividends is this: Each year, the business earns a profit (or net income). At the end of the year, the business can pay some or all of this to its stockholders. The amount that does get paid to stockholders is called dividends, and the amount that doesn't is the annual income retained in the business. Retained earnings is a part of stockholders' equity, the "OE" in the accounting equation A = L + OE.)
- Retained earnings. The retained earnings account tracks cumulative net income since the business began, minus cumulative dividends paid to stockholders since the business began.

Visual of statement of retained earnings in next section

Balance Sheet. A financial statement showing assets, liabilities, and owners' equity as of a *point* in time (e.g. 12/31/13).

- Assets. Stuff the business owns. Common assets:
    - Cash. Bank accounts, paper currency, coins, and checks.
    - Accounts receivable. IOU from customer (this is an asset to the business who's owed the money)
    - Notes receivable. *Written* IOU from another party (note: notes receivable are often like accounts receivable, which are IOUs from customers, except that with notes receivable the business holds a signed promissory note received from the owing party)

- Prepaid expenses (AKA deferred expenses). Items purchased but not yet used (e.g. prepaid rent, prepaid insurance)
- Long-Term Assets. Tangible (i.e. physical) assets, such as land, buildings, equipment, and furniture. These last longer than a year, and are *used in the operation of the business* (as *distinct* from inventory, which is held for resale).
    - Land. A "land" account keeps track of the historical cost of owned land (note: unlike other long-term assets such as buildings and vehicles, land is *not* depreciated)
    - Buildings. A "buildings" account keeps track of buildings owned (e.g. offices, warehouses, etc.)
    - Equipment, Furniture, and Fixtures. Items such as computer equipment, office equipment, store equipment, and furniture & fixtures. Businesses generally keep separate accounts for each item type.

- Liabilities. Debts of the company owed to others. Common liabilities:
    - Accounts payable. IOU to a supplier (vendor) (note: this is an asset to the business who's *owed* the money)
    - Notes payable. *Written* IOU to another party (note: notes payable are often like accounts payable, which are IOUs to suppliers, except that with notes payable the business signed a promissory note.

Notes payable can also represent money owed to a lender, such as a bank.)
  - Accrued liabilities. Liability for an expense incurred but not yet paid (e.g. taxes payable, interest payable, salaries payable)
- Stockholders' equity (also known as owners' equity). Amount of what is left over for business owners after total liabilities are subtracted from total assets (note: It may help to picture the accounting equation, A = L + OE.)
  - Common stock. Owner investments into the business (note: This is the part of Owners' Equity coming from what the stockholders invested in the business. Common Stock is a part of stockholders' equity, the "OE" in the accounting equation A = L + OE.)
  - Retained earnings. The retained earnings account tracks cumulative net income since the business began, minus cumulative dividends paid to stockholders since the business began. (Notes: net income equals revenues minus expenses. Another way to think of retained earnings is this: Each year, the business earns a profit (or net income). At the end of the year, the business can pay some or all of this to its stockholders. The amount that does get paid to stockholders is called dividends, and the amount that doesn't is added to existing retained earnings (if any). Retained earnings is a part of

stockholders' equity, the "OE" in the accounting equation A = L + OE.)

Visual of balance sheet in next section

Statement of Cash Flows. A financial statement showing sources and uses of cash over a given period.

- Operating Activities. Sources and uses of cash related to revenue and expense transactions. Essentially, cash paid to vendors and cash received from customers.
- Investing activities. Buying and selling long-term assets.
- Financial activities. Business-with-stockholder and Business-with-lender transactions (i.e. receiving cash from stockholders'; paying stockholders dividends; receiving cash from a lender; paying back lenders.)

Summary Diagrams

From Building Blocks of Financial Statements to Financial Statements

Transaction Narrative:

On 4/1/13, your business received $600 in its business checking account for legal services performed for a customer

General Journal

Date	Account	Debit	Credit
4/1/2013	Cash	600	
	Revenue		600

1. Copy amounts from journal (this page) to ledger (next page)
2. Copy ending balances from each ledger (next page) account to the trial balance (following page).
3. Copy trial balance numbers to the income statement, statement of retained earnings, and balance sheet (following page).
4. Notice that net income, which is used in the statement of retained earnings, is *not* taken from the trial balance directly, but rather is *calculated* on the income statement, as revenues minus expenses.

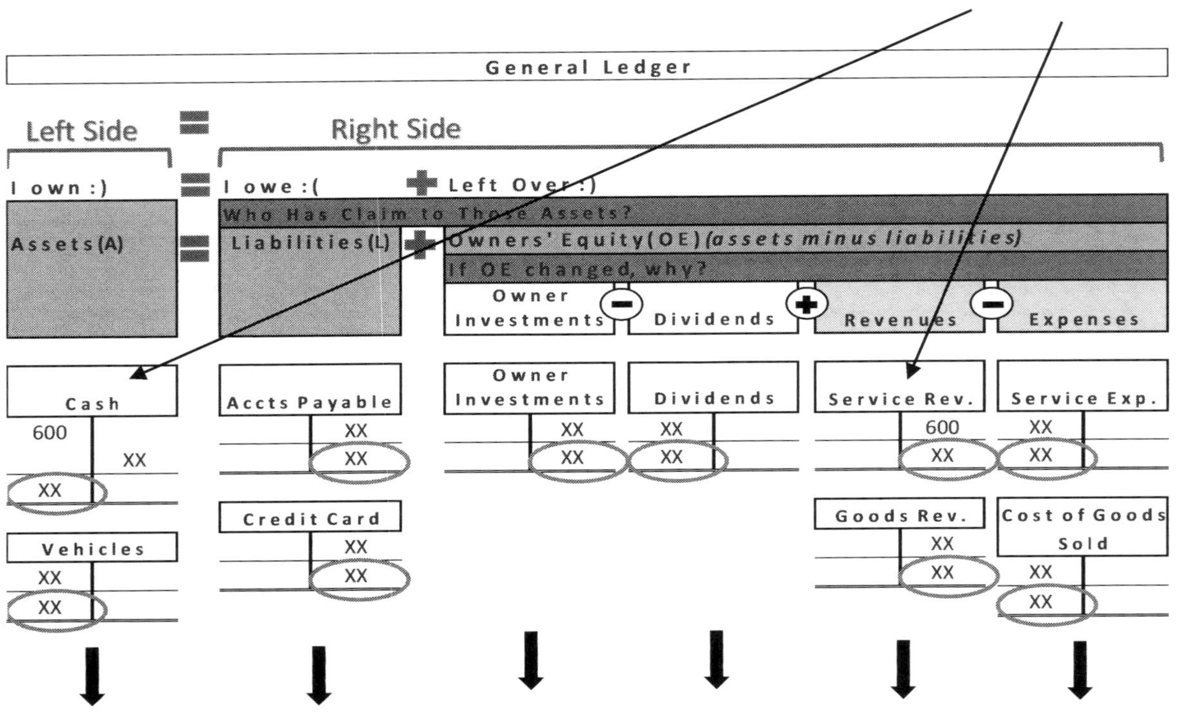
General Ledger
Left Side
Right Side
I own :)
I owe :(
Left Over :)
Assets(A)
Who Has Claim to Those Assets?
Liabilities(L)
Owners' Equity(OE) (assets minus liabilities)
If OE changed, why?
Owner Investments
Dividends
Revenues
Expenses
Cash
600
XX
XX
Vehicles
XX
XX
Accts Payable
XX
XX
Credit Card
XX
XX
Owner Investments
XX
XX
Dividends
XX
XX
Service Rev.
600
XX
Goods Rev.
XX
XX
Service Exp.
XX
XX
Cost of Goods Sold
XX
XX

ABC Company
Trial Balance (Before Closing Entries)
12/31/2013

Account Title	Balance	
	Debit	Credit
Assets:		
Cash	$XX	
Accounts receivable	XX	
Prepaid expenses	XX	
Vehicles	XX	
Buildings	XX	
Equipment	XX	
Liabilities:		
Accounts payable		$XX
Credit Card		XX
Unearned Revenue		XX
Equity:		
Common stock		XX
Dividends	XX	
Retained earnings		XX
Service Revenue		XX
Goods Revenue		XX
Service Expenses	XX	
Cost of Goods Sold	XX	
Total	XXX	XXX

ABC Company
Income Statement
1/1/13-12/31/13

Service Revenue	XX
Goods Revenue	XX
Total Revenue	XX
Service Expenses	XX
Cost of Goods Sold	XX
Total Expenses	XX
Net Income	XX

ABC Company
Statement of Retained Earnings
1/1/13-12/31/13

Beginning Retained Earnings	XX
Plus: Net Income	XX
Minus: Dividends	XX
Equals: Ending Retained Earnings	XX

ABC Company
Balance Sheet
12/31/2013

Assets:	
Cash	$XX
Accounts receivable	XX
Prepaid expenses	XX
Vehicles	XX
Buildings	XX
Equipment	XX
Total Assets	*XXX*
Liabilities:	
Accounts payable	XX
Credit Card	XX
Unearned Revenue	XX
Total Liabilities	*XX*
Equity:	
Common stock	XX
Retained earnings	XX
Total Equity	*XX*
Total Liabilities & Equity	*XXX*

About the Author

Logan Musil is an accounting professor at Florida State College at Jacksonville. He is a Certified Public Accountant (CPA) and holds a Bachelor's of Accounting and Master of Accountancy from the University of North Florida's AACSB Accredited College of Business. He has eight years of accounting and auditing experience, including extensive experience preparing and analyzing financial statements. He has experience auditing company financial statements for conformity with applicable financial reporting standards—evaluating audit evidence, performing analytic and detail tests on account balances, and evaluating test results in support of audit reports. In both the public and private sectors, he has enjoyed clarifying and simplifying accounting materials for the benefit of others.

You may find content by Logan on the Learn Basic Accounting Easy YouTube channel and at Udemy.com.

Printed in Great Britain
by Amazon